The Garden Indoors

by Jean Taylor and William Davidson

With drawings by Malcolm Drake

STANLEY PAUL/LONDON

STANLEY PAUL LIMITED
178–202 Great Portland Street, London W1

AN IMPRINT OF THE HUTCHINSON GROUP

London Melbourne Sydney
Auckland Johannesburg Cape Town
and agencies throughout the world

First published February 1971
Second Impression April 1971

This book has been set in Bembo type, printed in Great Britain
by offset litho at Taylor Garnett Evans & Co. Ltd,
Watford, Herts.

ISBN 0 09 107151 8

Contents

(*Pot Luck* and *Today's Living* have been written by William Davidson. All other chapters are by Jean Taylor)

Introduction

Flowers and plants are lovely to have anywhere—in churches, offices, schools, shops, hotels and particularly in the home. They enhance their surroundings and soften the furnishings with their natural beauty. By drawing attention to themselves they quite often draw the eye away from shabbiness and awkward architectural features. They can conceal ugly views. Sometimes they provide a needed colour link between furnishings or give a bright accent in a drab room. Foliage plants are valuable for their sculptural form and long lives, and nothing can match flowers for colour impact.

Arranging flowers and caring for plants are enjoyable occupations in themselves. They can be a creative interest, a relief from the tensions of the world and even a solace in difficult times. Many plants are very easy to grow and flowers need not take much time and trouble to arrange, unless you want them to: but they never fail to reward you.

This book describes the simple skills necessary for growing and displaying plants; suggests how to buy plants and flowers; how to prepare flowers so that they last well in the house; how to preserve plant material for winter use; how to use wood, fruit shells and figurines with flowers so that only a few are needed; and gives guides for making attractive designs.

With a knowledge of these simple basic skills bringing the garden indoors should never be anything but a pleasure.

JEAN TAYLOR

I

Pot Luck

THE NEED FOR PLANTS

Over the past twenty-five years the demand for indoor plants has increased enormously, and in this time the available range has been much extended and the quality improved. The days are long past since all you could expect was the aspidistra, palm and a selection of ferns. We can now walk into any good flower shop and see a variety of plants that would not have seemed possible a few years ago.

Though we have some way to go in order to catch up on our Continental neighbours, plants are gradually becoming an essential part of our every day lives. We see them in railway stations, hotels, shops and offices, as well as in people's homes. In fact, office plants have become so popular that designers are dispensing with conventional interior walls as a means of sub-dividing floor space and are substituting foliage plants instead.

Many people feel that they must have growing things around them and, it goes without saying, that living plants by their nature do most to give life to a room.

PLANT SELECTION

Not only are indoor plants attractive in themselves, but growing them can become a fascinating hobby. So it is well to begin on the right foot if one is to avoid disappointment. The beginner may well be tempted, on entering the florist's shop, to select the most colourful and exotic plant on display, but this is almost sure to prove to be unwise in a comparatively short space of time. Generally speaking, the more colourful the foliage the more difficult the plant is likely to be to cultivate. There are, of course, a few exceptions to this rule, and the humble and easily grown coleus, with its gaily coloured foliage, is probably the best example.

Seek the advice of your florist or nurseryman supplier in the first instance, or check the plant label which will in most instances indicate whether or not the plant is easy or difficult to care for.

Bear in mind that it is infinitely more satisfying to see a simple plant growing well in average conditions rather than witness the decline of an exotic and difficult plant in the same environment.

Buying Plants The actual place of purchase is also worthy of consideration, particularly during the winter months when plants can so easily succumb to the low temperatures to which they may be exposed between leaving the nursery and getting to their eventual home. Since carrying home an unwrapped plant over even a short distance can often prove fatal during the cold days of winter, one should insist on proper wrapping when buying a delicate foliage plant. Also, one should avoid the supplier who does not adequately protect his plants, not only during the winter but on colder days at other times of the year.

As interest in house plants increases there is an ever wider range of tradesmen willing to stock and sell them. The result is that they may be bought from the street trader, door-to-door salesman, conventional flower shop, or in the grand department store. Whoever the supplier may be, the buyer should always select plants with firm healthy leaves, and avoid any plants that have marked or limp leaves, which are an indication of mismanagement on the part of the stockist or his supplier.

PLANTS FOR SITUATIONS

Light Adequate light is absolutely essential for healthy plants.

However much one may feel that a pot plant would be perfect for brightening up the dark corner it must be realised that the improvement would only be for a very limited period, as the majority of plants quickly deteriorate in inadequate light.

This is not to say that all plants should be crammed on to the windowsill and subjected to the full intensity of any sunlight that may be about. Far from it; very few of our house plants will survive unscathed in the blistering heat of the sun when it is magnified by the glass window pane. Most of the cacti and succulents will tolerate long periods of direct sunlight, but these do not, strictly speaking, come under the general category of house plants.

Possibly the most durable of all the house plants is *Sansevieria trifasciata Laurentii* (more easily recognised by its amusing common name of Mother-in-Law's Tongue) which thrives on the sunny windowsill. The worst enemies of this plant are wet and cold, and a combination of both will almost invariably prove to be fatal. A moderate amount of water (every ten to fourteen days, less in winter) and a minimum temperature in the region of 55/60°F (13/16°C) is all that is needed to succeed with this member of the lily family. It really does seem to thrive on neglect.

Ivies with variegated leaves, *Chlorophytum commosum Variegatum* (Spider Plant) and the variegated *Peperomias* are others that will tolerate quite sunny conditions.

In fact, though it very often depends on the particular variety, I have found that many of the *Saintpaulias* (African Violets), which are generally considered to be difficult, do perfectly well in the sunny window provided the sun does

(*Left*) Sansevieria trifasciata Laurentii (Mother-in-law's tongue)
(*right*) Bowl of house plants

not become excessively bright. There is one very important precaution here however; no water should be allowed to get onto flowers or leaves when watering, otherwise unsightly blotches on leaves and discoloured flowers will result.

Of course, even though plants may be recommended for a sunny window position this does not necessarily mean that they will fare better if subjected to continual full sunlight—no harm will be done if on the hottest days plants are removed to a cooler part of the room. Though it may appear untidy, plants can be temporarily protected from the sun by covering them over with a sheet of newspaper.

For some plants it is absolutely essential that they should enjoy maximum sunlight if they are to retain their attractive colouring—the Croton, or Codiaeum is one of these. Commonly known as Joseph's Coat, there are *Crotons* available in almost every colour of the rainbow, and quite often almost all these colours may be seen on the same plant.

Shade For the shadier situation, not dark, we could quote almost ad lib from the house plant growers' catalogues, as almost all plants offered for sale are suited to this sort of position, provided of course that the temperature is correct for the particular plant.

Doubtless, the most important family of plants as far as the house plant grower is concerned is the one to which the common Lords-and-Ladies belongs—*Araceae*. Almost all the plants in this family prefer a shady situation; some are comparatively easy to care for, while others will test the skill of the most competent grower with ideal conditions at his disposal. I would like to illustrate and emphasise this point; some years ago I met a gardener who said that his Scottish head gardener once offered him ten shillings for every perfect leaf of *Alocasia indica* that he could grow—alas, he collected nothing from his canny and knowledgeable chief.

In the *Araceae* family the philodendrons (which are mostly green in colour) have leaves with an infinite variety of shapes from the heart shaped *P. scandens* to the radiating leaves of *P. bipinnatifidium*. *Monstera deliciosa* (Swiss Cheese Plant) is the best known of the aroids and is among the most majestic of our indoor plants. Like most of his relatives the monstera requires a temperature in the region of 65°F (18°C) if it is to do well. In lower temperatures it is usual for plants to produce entire leaves instead of the more attractive leaves that are normal. In particularly good conditions plants will in time produce leaves with perforated centres as well as serrated edges.

A word of warning here about one of the plants in the aroid family, the dieffenbachia. These are available in several varieties, of which *D. exotica* and *D. 'pia'* are probably best indoors. Many of our house plants have easily remembered common names, and that given to the dieffenbachia is Dumb Cane, for a special reason. Should the sap of this plant inadvertently find its way into one's mouth the tongue will swell up and make speech impossible for several days, hence the name Dumb Cane. However, the stem when cut gives off such an unpleasant odour, that contact with the tongue is unlikely. All the same, do be particularly careful with dieffenbachias when there are children around.

One of the few plants that seem to do reasonably well in the darker more difficult position is the favourite of our Victorian forbears, *Aspidistra lurida* (aptly named the Cast Iron Plant). It seems to put up with any sort of ill treatment, and one hears that it is again returning to favour with exorbitant prices of 10/- per leaf quoted as a purchase price. However, at the risk of offending some readers, I must say that I cannot myself imagine that the aspidistra will return to its former place of eminence when there are so many more colourful and more reasonably priced plants to choose from.

Both Light and Shade Some of our house plants serve a dual purpose in respect of light and shade, in that they will do almost equally well in either situation; the colouring of many species will dictate the sort of position they prefer. For example, ivies with variegated leaves will retain their attractive colouring better in lighter conditions, while those with green leaves, such as *Hedera chicago* and *H. green ripple* will fare better out of direct sunlight.

WATERING

The watering of indoor plants is one of the grower's most important functions, but it is also one of the most difficult subjects on which to give satisfactory advice. Although I have spent most of my working life looking after, and instructing others how to look after plants, I still find it almost impossible to instil into some employees exactly what is required in the way of watering. Some people have a natural aptitude for this apparently simple task (perhaps they have "greenfingers"), while others never quite grasp what is needed. So, how do we instruct simply by means of the written word?

Firstly, let it be said that there is a vast difference between watering plants which grow quickly in a greenhouse and the relatively slow growing indoor plants. The most important consideration when watering house plants, with just a few exceptions, is to ensure that they never become too wet. This is particularly important between October and March when plants put on little, if any, new growth.

Rather than immerse plants in buckets of water for specified lengths of time I find there is better control over watering if it is done by filling the space between the surface of the compost and the rim of the pot each time one waters. If the pot has been overfilled with compost it will do no harm if a little compost is removed in order to provide a space for watering. If the compost is very dry the space can be filled a second time. I frequently stress the dangers of overwatering plants, but it must also be borne in mind that damage can be equally harmful if the compost becomes excessively dry. Remember that there should at no time be a gap between the compost and the sides of the pot. This harmful situation is brought about by allowing the compost to become so dry that it shrinks.

Many of the more tender plants will benefit from being watered with tepid water, and none will be harmed by using water that has had the chill taken off. This doesn't mean that you must boil a kettle in order to get tepid water. Just leave a canful in a warm room overnight and it will be fine for using in the morning. If clean rain water is available it will be all the more beneficial to many house plants; on the other hand, do not use water that has come through a water softening unit.

Earlier in this chapter I mentioned that some plants are exceptions to the general rule of 'never too much water'. Here are three of them. The indoor azalea (*A. indica*) must never be allowed to dry out, and benefits considerably if there is an alternative to hard tap water. *Aphelandra brockfield*, the silver and green leaved plant with exotic yellow bracts, usually available throughout the summer months, is another plant that must be kept moist at all times. And the hydrangea when in active growth fares better if copiously watered.

A florist acquaintance told me a true story that made me almost despair of ever getting any sort of sanity into the business of watering. A customer took back to this florist a philodendron that was very dead and bone dry. Questioned about the dryness of the plant, the customer replied by saying that the plant was watered every day. At this the florist incredulously asked, 'How much?' and was answered, 'Three drops every day, one for the Father, one for the Son and one for the Holy Ghost'.

FEED AND POT

Feeding The actual brand of fertiliser used for feeding pot plants is not too important provided it is a properly balanced product, and not some concoction that one might mix together from whatever is available in the potting shed. The really important consideration here is that use of a fertiliser is absolutely essential if plants are to survive and grow indoors. So even if the plant you are buying is the first and only one in your possession, you should buy a fertiliser of some kind at the same time as you buy the plant.

It can generally be assumed that all plants will have been fed regularly before they are despatched from the nursery, and if this source of nutrition should suddenly cease it is natural and inevitable that the plants will deteriorate.

There are just a few basic rules when applying fertiliser:

never feed a dry plant, feed only during the growing season, and abide by the makers' instructions. Giving two or three times the recommended amount does not mean that the plant will do that much better. Never feed a sick plant: sick plants are better kept on the dry side in a warm room to encourage fresh root development, as root failure (often due to over-watering) is one of the most common reasons for plants taking on a sickly appearance.

Overfeeding, overwatering and overpotting of plants are three common reasons for failure—let moderation be the watchword.

Potting Most indoor plants look better and are often healthier if kept in relatively small pots, provided that feeding is regularly attended to. But the time must come, nonetheless, when plants will require potting-on into a larger container. For active plants that have put on a reasonable amount of new growth during the previous growing season, re-potting should take place about every second year.

The actual potting operation is something that the inexperienced plant owner approaches with a certain amount of trepidation. For encouragement and comfort, there are a few basic potting-on rules.

Firstly, pot early in the year. Sometime in April is ideal, since plants then have a full growing season ahead of them. Secondly, the new pot should be only a little larger than the one from which the plant is being transferred. Thirdly, there should be about one inch of space between the old root ball and the new pot.

For indoor plants the compost must be light and spongy, into such a mixture the delicate young roots will more easily penetrate. Though all manner of composts can be suggested, I invariably get good results from a mixture composed of $\frac{2}{3}$ John Innes potting compost No. 2 (No. 3 for larger plants) and $\frac{1}{3}$ peat; if peat is not available, leafmould

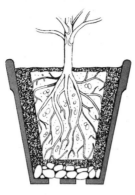

Potting on

may be used as a substitute.

The majority of clay pots are provided with a single drainage hole, so a piece of broken pot (a crock) should be placed over this hole before putting any compost into the pot; this will ensure that the hole does not become blocked, so obstructing drainage. Water should quite quickly drain through the compost, and pots that are slow to drain should have the rootball removed so that the crock can be inspected. If the drainage hole is blocked the crock should be removed and cleaned before being replaced. Modern plastic pots are well supplied with holes through which excess moisture can drain away, so there is no need for these to be crocked.

To simplify potting-on for the beginner (it may even suit the expert!) it will be an easier task if an empty pot, the same size as the one in which the plant is growing, is potted into the new compost in order to form a mould. It is then a simple operation to remove the plant from its pot and pop it into the ready made hole. It is essential that the compost remains open in texture, so it is important to remember when potting that the compost ought to be gently firmed into position with finger pressure only, and must on no account be rammed hard.

When the potting operation has been completed the compost should be watered in order to allow it to settle down, and thereafter it should be kept on the dry side for about ten days after which more frequent watering can be given. Keeping the compost on the dry side to begin with will induce young roots to forage for moisture in the new mixture. It is also important to ensure that the plant about to be re-potted is well watered before being removed from its first pot.

GENERAL APPEARANCE

Washing Almost all the plants used for indoor decoration will benefit from having their faces washed periodically—like the furniture surrounding them, they become dusty and need occasional attention. On average, plants should have their leaves cleaned thoroughly once every three months, and the majority will take on a much brighter appearance if wiped over regularly with a soft damp cloth. Hard rubbing is not necessary. There are proprietary leaf cleaning agents available, but it is usually wise to experiment on one or two leaves to begin with, so as to find out what the plant's reaction will be, since some plants are allergic to almost any form of chemical being rubbed onto their leaves. When cleaning plants one must avoid touching tender young leaves and this applies particularly to *Ficus robusta* (the Rubber Plant) and the monstera.

Also, when contemplating a spring clean of plants' foliage, care must be taken not to clean those with hairy or downy leaves. A few examples of such plants are the saintpaulias, platycerium, *Begonia rex* and *B. masoniana* (Iron Cross). Some of the pileas are also likely to suffer damage in this way. Much of the dust on hairy leaved plants can be removed by gently cleaning it with a soft brush.

Pests If plants are clean and healthy when bought, pests do not cause much bother. However, you are almost sure at some time or other to find greenfly on your plants. The best

15

way to control this pest is to spray plants thoroughly with a suitable insecticide, obtainable from any gardening shop. When spraying, pay particular attention to the undersides of leaves, and take plants out into the garden to treat them.

Scale insects are sometimes troublesome; these are small black or brown insects that attach themselves to the undersides of leaves and stems and look not unlike miniature limpets. A sponge soaked in insecticide can be used gently to wipe them off plants. Always use rubber gloves and wash hands after using any insecticide.

Mealy bugs can be dealt with by touching them with methylated spirits; mealy bugs resemble small woodlice and are a downy white in colour.

Red spider is checked by spraying the undersides of leaves with suitable insecticide; dry brown leaves are an indication of their presence. Spraying undersides of leaves is absolutely essential if any measure of control is to be achieved.

PLANTS AND CENTRAL HEATING

Central heating is often blamed by people who have failed to grow plants indoors, and where excessively hot dry conditions prevail it is a valid reason for failure. But central heating at a constant controlled temperature in the 68/70°F (18/21°C) range should present few problems to the majority of plants, other than ivies and such like, which prefer lower temperatures.

A Moist Atmosphere The dry atmosphere of centrally heated rooms is the real bugbear, so something must be done to counteract these dry conditions by providing a little moist atmosphere around the plants. Spraying foliage periodically is one way, though damp leaves do seem to attract dust and spoil the appearance of plants to some extent.

Possibly the best method of providing moisture is to group plants together in a watertight container of some kind. The container is filled with moist peat into which

Plants grouped

plant-pots are plunged *to their rims only*. If pots are *buried* there will be problems when watering, as it will be impossible to see whether or not the compost in the pot is wet or dry. By keeping the peat permanently moist there will always be a moist feeling around the plants.

Alternatively a tray can be used. The tray must be shallow but at the same time deep enough to take an inch layer of pebbles or moist sand on which the plants are then placed. The pebbles or sand must be kept moist, but care must be taken to make quite sure that the plant-pots do not actually stand in water, as this is fatal to almost all indoor plants.

Dry atmosphere is also the reason why plants suspended in wall containers in centrally heated rooms seldom do well. One might also add that plants in wall containers placed immediately above radiators have absolutely no chance of survival. Life is also made difficult for plants on window-ledges with radiators underneath. To counteract the effect of hot air rising through the foliage of plants on window ledges, the width of the window ledge should be extended over the radiator so that hot air is directed *above* rather than *through* the foliage.

Fluctuating Temperatures The wildly fluctuating temperatures in rooms heated by clock control mechanism also present problems. Here plants are being baked in temperatures in the eighties at eleven p.m. and chilled to fifty or less in the middle of the night. Remedies are difficult to suggest for such conditions but probably the best solution is to buy only the more tolerant house plants—sansevierias, rhoicissus and *philodendron scandens* being three of the most durable.

Gas Heating It will be found that with some forms of gas heating, plants will be difficult to grow indoors. This is particularly the case with flowering plants, which will be reluctant to produce flowers for a second time. In these conditions plants with thicker leaves seem to do best.

SIMPLE PROPAGATION

The plant grower who raises an extra large specimen or rears a difficult plant to perfection naturally takes a justifiable pride in his achievement, but this is nothing to compare with the pride he feels when he can claim to have raised the plant he is displaying *from a cutting*. Certainly, raising one's own plants provides a deal of satisfaction, particularly if it is done on the windowsill with no sophisticated aids whatever.

Many of our house plants can be increased with very little bother, and two of these which spring immediately to mind are the chlorophytum (Spider Plant) and *saxifrage sarmentosa* (Mother-of-Thousands). Both these plants produce small plantlets in much the same way as strawberry runners. To propogate them requires simply the provision of small pots filled with a peaty compost into which young plantlets are pegged down with a hairpin or piece of bent wire. When plantlets are obviously growing away they can be severed from the parent plant and allowed to develop individually. Under normal conditions young plants grow more quickly and look fresher than the parents from which they originated. Consequently it is wise policy to propagate fresh plants every second or third year and to discard the older, less attractive

Chlorophytum propogation

plant. The best plants are produced from the best cuttings, so when selecting material for propagating one must sacrifice the best pieces from the originals, and not the tired half-dead pieces.

In a Polythene Bag It is possible to put plants into a polythene bag in order to keep them moist and, in effect, to make a miniature greenhouse for them. When propagating young plants, the polythene bag, being completely airtight, will almost eliminate transpiration, and so ensure that cuttings do not dry out but remain firm while roots are being produced.

Most of the smaller leaved plants can be rooted quite satisfactorily inside a polythene bag. This applies particularly to the ivies, tradescantias, peperomias and saintpaulias. Ivies are simply done by cutting firm stems into sections with two leaves attached, and placing five or six around the edge of a small pot filled with almost any reasonable compost. Putting several cuttings in each pot ensures that a full, bushy plant is produced rather than the spindly result of using a single cutting.

Tradescantias are done in much the same way, but cuttings in this case should be taken from the topmost three or four inches of growth. Though it is not essential it is customary to remove one or two of the lower leaves of tradescantias before inserting them in the compost. Select the best coloured pieces and avoid green cuttings.

From Leaves Peperomias caperata and hederafolia are propagated in much the same way as saintpaulias by removing individual leaves and standing them upright in peaty compost. Leaves should be inserted just far enough for them to remain erect. To prevent damage to the leaf stalk it is wise to dibble a hole with a pencil just deep enough to receive the cutting.

In Water Though a peaty compost or one of the proprietary soilless mixtures is advised for propagating purposes there is no reason why many of the house plant cuttings should not be started in water. This is done by suspending the cuttings in a narrow-necked bottle filled with water. Having produced roots in water, cuttings must be potted carefully into small pots filled with one of the recommended potting composts.

Saintpaulias A word about saintpaulia cuttings. I often listen to comments about saintpaulias which grow into clumpy plants that push flowers and leaves out in all directions and seldom look attractive. This results from mismanagement during the cutting stage of the plant's existence. Careful inspection of young plantlets that are just beginning to grow will show that they are in fact a cluster of individual plants, which if left to develop in this way will become relatively unattractive.

In order to produce saintpaulias with a flat effect that have flowers standing away from the foliage in the centre of the plant, it is important that clumps of young plants be carefully teased apart when they are large enough to handle. Young plants, usually with two leaves, are then planted up individually with the result that all leaves as they are produced will radiate from a central crown, with flowers standing cleanly away from the leaves.

PLANTS ON HOLIDAY

Knowing what to do with pot plants at holiday times can

present problems. However, I feel that the problems of holiday care for plants are somewhat exaggerated. Over short absences of a week, or even ten days, plants will not suffer unduly if they are well watered just before being left. It is, however, wise to remove plants from sunny positions in order to minimise drying out. Many plants benefit as a result of the short respite from the attentions of the over zealous plant owner and his or her watering can, but the needs of plants must be attended to immediately on return from holiday.

Capillary Watering Units There are several ways of overcoming the problem of longer absence, and use of one of the many proprietary capillary watering units (or self-watering pots) is probably the most satisfactory answer. These can be bought as ready-made units that only need filling with water at about monthly intervals.

A simpler and cheaper unit can be improvised by filling a basin or old baking tin with wet sand. Plant pots are then

THREE METHODS OF CARING FOR PLANTS WHEN ON HOLIDAY
(*left to right*) Enclosing the pot in polythene; a self-watering pot; the plant enclosed in a polythene bag

well watered before being pressed gently into the surface of the sand. Plastic pots are perfect for this purpose as they have thin bases and many drainage holes which ensure that pot compost and sand come into immediate contact and this in turn ensures that water is drawn up from the sand into the pot by capillary action. If clay pots are used for this purpose it is important that the drainage hole in the bottom of the pot is plugged with a piece of cotton wool or similar material to give the necessary contact between sand and compost.

Polythene Bags Another cheap and simple method of caring for plants during any absence is to enclose the entire plant and pot in an airtight polythene bag, which will restrict transpiration and keeps plants reasonably moist. Place three evenly spaced stakes around the plant so that when they are pushed into the compost they are slightly taller than the plant, so as to prevent the polythene from sagging around the leaves and causing them to rot. When the plant is placed in the bag the top should be securely tied to make sure that no air is allowed to escape. This method provides what amounts to a miniature individual greenhouse for each plant. Similarly for short periods a polythene bag can be tied around the pot at the base of the stem of the plant, again slowing up the drying-out process.

Neighbours Having mentioned these various ways of caring for plants while on holiday, I still feel that the reliable neighbour who is prepared to care for plants is often the most satisfactory answer.

However, a word of caution here. Don't just appear on your neighbour's doorstep, deliver the plants and depart. Having got to know almost the exact requirements of your plants over the years it is a simple task to stick a piece of white adhesive paper on each pot with written instructions giving the exact amount of water and fertiliser needed.

2

Todays Living

THE CONTINENTAL INFLUENCE

In the good old days it was not unusual for the blemished wallpaper or defective bit of dad's decorating to be hidden behind a conveniently placed picture. It might be said that indoor plants are used for the same purpose today but in fact, modern house plants perform a much more important function, as the most fleeting visit to the Continent makes abundantly clear.

On the Continent the foliage plant has become very much an integral part of everyday life and not something that perches precariously on an inadequate windowsill, or hangs forlornly from an ill-positioned wall attachment. Our Continental neighbours have had a twenty year start on us as far as culture and appreciation of house plants is concerned, and we have a long way to go to catch up with them.

In Holland there appears to be what amounts to competition among neighbours to see who can provide the best display of indoor plants, in much the same way as we have garden competitions in this country. This sort of life has been described as a 'goldfish bowl existence', our Dutch neighbours not seeming to share our insular desire for privacy. The majority of living rooms are on view for all to see in the evening, and very beautiful they look with their diffused lighting and astonishing displays of exotic foliage plants. For some reason the Stagshorn Fern (*Platycerium alcicorne*) seems to become more and more popular in Holland, while in Germany almost every window sports what look like endless lines of Mother-in-Law's Tongues (sansevieria).

It is quite usual to find that modern Continental homes have been designed with plants in mind. Windowsills instead of being a paltry few inches wide are often two feet wide and capable of accommodating a dozen or more plants of reasonable size. Many of these windowsills are tiled over and waterproofed, with a drainage plug which allows surplus water to drain away outside, so preventing any mess on carpets when watering.

Another reason, I feel sure, for indoor plants doing so well in Continental homes is that there is usually a minimum of drapery in the way of curtaining at windows. Especially where rooms have large picture windows, this ensures that plants have adequate light in almost any position in the room.

Also, the skilful use of interior lighting over and around plants further assists their growth, and enhances their appearance. In this country at the moment there are many experiments taking place with growing-rooms in which plants are

Plants on a window-sill

successfully reared entirely in artificial light. For many years in America and in England the more enthusisiatic saintpaulia growers have been raising plants in cellars and rooms fitted out with specialised fluorescent lighting, though ordinary lighting will give quite good results. It is important to ensure that lights are left on for a period of some ten to twelve hours each day.

When using high intensity lights, particularly spotlighting, it is important that plants should be kept far enough away from the heat of lamps to prevent foliage becoming scorched.

EFFECTIVE DISPLAY

Harking back to the Continental influence, I would say that effective display in the average living room is a combination of diffused lighting and carefully positioned plants. Needless to say, plants that are to be really effective when thus 'lit up' must be not only attractive in themselves but of reasonable quality. Yellow, dying and drooping leaves have very little appeal, to put it mildly

Grouping For indoor decoration I favour the grouping of plants on tables or in large containers of some kind, whether these are ornamental wrought iron troughs or simple wooden boxes. Possibly the simplest method of setting off plants in a group is on the small table, or trolley. The latter is ideal, as plants can be put near the window in the light during the day and can be brought into the room in the evening where they will be warmer.

Plants may also be taken from their pots and freely planted in smaller ornamental containers, though this method does restrict the choice of plants to those that require similar treatment in the way of watering and such like. Where plants of differing moisture requirements are planted together, sanseveiria and philodendron for example, it is usually better to err on the side of dryness when watering. This also

A group of plants on a table

applies to containers that have no drainage holes and as a result there is a likelihood of compost becoming saturated if water is not given sparingly.

Lighting Where possible, it will be found that artificial lighting positioned above plants will improve the appearance of the display quite remarkably, and it will also benefit plants generally. Even individual plants will look very much better if a light is placed over them.

SPECIMEN PLANTS

For more spacious surroundings there is quite a wide variety of plants available in specimen sizes—these are quite capable of holding their own as individuals and need not be grouped together unless a really grand display is contemplated. The following is a selection of plants that may either be bought as specimens, or may be grown on to become large plants.

Monstera deliciosa This is a comparatively easy plant that should be kept moist though never saturated. Frequent feeding with weak liquid fertiliser is preferable to occasional large doses.

Philodendrons The varieties *P. hastatum*, *P. Burgundy* and *P. bipinnatifidium* in time take on a quite majestic appearance. The first two will grow more rapidly and healthily if a moist central support can be provided for aerial roots to grow into. The simplest way of doing this is to bind a thick layer of sphagnum moss along the length of a stout cane with plastic-covered wire. If the moss is kept permanently moist the aerial roots will quickly work their way into it. The monstera may also be treated in similar fashion.

Dracaena A particular favourite of mine, *Dracaena marginata* is a costly plant on account of its slow rate of growth, but ideal in almost any surroundings. The stark, spikey leaves of a few plants grouped together present a very pleasing picture. It is quite natural for plants to shed lower leaves as they increase in height, but this is no drawback with dracaena as the attraction is in tufted leaves supported by slender stems, giving a palm like appearance.

Ficus The *Ficus robusta*, an improvement on the old *F. decora* will in time attain tree proportions, and at a height of about six-feet, side growths usually develop from the axils of the topmost leaves, giving the plant a branching and often more handsome look. Slightly more delicate, *F. lyrata* has leaves shaped like the body of a violin, hence the common name of Fiddle-leaved fig. Higher temperature in the region of 66°F (18°C), is required for this one. The weeping fig, *F. benjamina*, has quite a different appearance, with smaller leaves on elegantly drooping stems. A settling-in period is usually needed for the *benjamina*, as it frequently loses some of its leaves before becoming adjusted to its new environment.

Pandanus Veitchii. Pandanus Veitchii never has been very plentiful, and keen demand has made it a scarce commodity. Straplike leaves, green and white in colour, have spiteful saw edges, so it is important that plants should be positioned out of harms way. Kept on the dry side in good light with moderate temperature, it will give little trouble. It is an ideal plant for providing a change of leaf form as well as colour.

Scheffleria Digitata Excellent as an individual plant, *Scheffleria digitata* has green nine-lobed leaves that stand stiffly away from the main stem of the plant on petioles up to two feet in length. A minimum temperature of 66°F (18°C) is needed. If roots are given a free run in a larger container the scheffleria grows rapidly to a height of some twelve to fifteen feet, but there is little fear of such development in the average home, though it is quite a possibility in the spacious office entrance hall.

Climbers Many of the smaller plants that are natural climbers may also be bought as, or grown-on to become specimen plants. The best and most durable natural climbing indoor plant is *Rhoicissus rhomboidea* (the Grape Ivy). In the same family, *Cissus antarctica* is also a fairly rapid growing plant, but a little more temperamental. *Philodendron scandens* is another plant that can be encouraged to become reasonably tall.

Ivies In the ivy family (araliaceae) *Hedera canariensis* is quick growing and improves for being grown against either a trellis or canes arranged in fan shape. In the same family, the fatshedera is useful where a tall, slender plant is wanted. A warning here—chemical cleaning agents should not be used to clean these leaves as they are particularly susceptible to damage.

Plants in the intermediate sizes (two to four feet in height) are always in demand as they are ideal for planting in office containers where minimum care is important because it reduces maintenance costs. Plants of this size are either in 5 inch (13 cm.) pots or 7 inch (18 cm.) pots, so require much less frequent watering than smaller pots that dry out much more rapidly.

Among the intermediates we get the usual crop of ficuses, ivies, philodendrons, vines (*rhoicissus* and *C. antartica*) and monsteras. However, there are also a number of more unusual plants to choose from.

Croton The croton family provides a selection of plants in an infinite range of colours, but they are difficult to care for as they require very hot, humid conditions in order to be at their best. Keep moist, feed and place in full sun to retain colouring; when in the shade plants quickly revert to green and tend to lose lower leaves. The croton is a plant for the expert or the person who can afford to enjoy its beauty for a few months and then expect to see it deteriorate. Flower arrangers find the crotons fascinating, so presumably a few falling leaves may be a blessing in disguise.

Dracaena. Dracaena deremensisis, a little easier to care for than the croton, has grey and green leaves, and is another plant that may interest the flower arranger. It needs similar treatment to that suggested for the croton, but it should not be placed in such a sunny position. The Flaming Dragon Tree (to give it its common name), *Dracaena terminalis* firebrand has bright cerise-coloured leaves that fade to a dull red as the plant ages. It is a truly remarkable plant, and surely one of the most colourful pot plants offered for sale. Good light is needed and rain water is a decided advantage when watering. The maximum height for this plant is about two feet.

Ficus. *Ficus diversifolia*, a plant of outstanding charm with small rounded leaves on graceful stems, has as its main attraction masses of berries which are ever present. No special treatment is required other than keeping the compost moist and avoiding cold conditions.

Sansevieria The sansevieria, though sold in large quantities as small plants, is at its best when seen growing in five or seven inch pots. Stout leaves often three feet in length are then produced. Also, larger plants flower regularly during the summer months. The flowers themselves are not particularly attractive, but have a pleasant though fleeting scent when they first open. This is the one plant which really does seem to thrive on neglect, needing very little water or feeding.

(*Left*) Croton
(*right*) Ficus robusta

Citrus. Citrus mitis, the miniature fruiting orange tree, in spite of its cost is much sought after by those who prefer something really exotic and out of the ordinary. Exceptional plants of these small citrus may have as many as 150 perfectly shaped small oranges on plants no more than three feet in height. It must be stressed, however, that this would be an exceptional number. Maximum sunlight during the summer months is essential, so place plants out of doors in a sheltered spot where they catch all the sun that is going. The comparatively delicate root system will not tolerate strong feeding—fertiliser is best given very weak with each watering. This citrus which bears fruit and flowers at the same time is a very fine sight indeed.

COMPACT AND TRAILING PLANTS

There are masses of these, so I will only mention a few of the newer plants and some of my own particular favourites.

Pilea Urticaceae, a much neglected family of plants, provides us with the compact and attractive pileas. Two that have come to the fore in recent years are *P*. 'Norfolk' and *P*. Moon Valley'. The former is a pleasant plant with bronze coloured foliage that will take on a pinkish shade if placed in good light. The latter is a more attractive plant in its habit of growth, and has colouring very similar to that of the Iron Cross begonia, *B. masoniana*, and seems to blend in with almost any colour scheme. Both these are good windowsill plants as they occupy little space and do not get in the way of curtains and such like.

Rex Begonia The *rex begonias* are well known for their colourful foliage, and are reasonably easy to care for during the summer months, although they require careful attention and warm conditions in winter, when water must be given sparingly. (This treatment applies equally to almost all the plants grown indoors). *B. cleopatra* is a more recent introduction to the house plant range and is a particularly easy plant to care for. If watering is kept to the minimum (I water my plant thoroughly once every two weeks, less in winter) and if very little fertiliser is given, the leaves will be smaller, more colourful and much more attractive.

Peperomias Peperomias generally are excellent plants for bowls, pot-et-fleur and smaller arrangements. One of my special favourites has a rather unpronounceable name, *P. tithymaloides*, which has masses of trailing cream and green leaves. *P. magnolaefolia* has similar colouring and stiffer foliage—both are easy to care for.

Bromeliads Bromeliads are available in all sorts of lovely colours and many of the plants bear the most exotic flowers imaginable. The pineapple belongs to this family of plants and almost all of them are easy to care for. Water is given by filling the central urn-like part of the plant when necessary —very little water is needed in the actual compost. One of the best known Bromeliads is *Aechmea rhodocyanea*, which has grey foliage and small blue flowers, but the main attraction is the magnificent pink bract which emerges from the water in the centre and may remain colourful for up to twelve months from the time it first appears.

Ivies The ivies are also indispensable as trailing plants for adding the final touch to arrangements, especially when breaking the line of a table edge, or container rim. For toughness *hedera Glacier* is the best variegated one, but by far the most attractive is *H. adam*. Its very tiny, perfectly shaped grey and white leaves that almost overlap one another as they grow are a real joy.

Grevillea and Dizygothica These are two very graceful small plants that in time grow to become quite substantial. (*Dizygotheca elegantissima* is also sold as *Aralia elegantissima*), The grevillia is much the easiest to grow and has an upright habit and soft green leaves. *D. elegantissima* is indeed elegant as the name suggests and has foliage that is almost black in colour on well grown plants, an excellent plant in rooms where the décor is very light. It is more difficult to care for, though, and abhors wet, cold conditions during the winter months.

SEASONAL PLANTS

Strictly speaking the term 'House Plant' applies to foliage plants that are a permanent part of house decoration, but it would all be rather dull if we could not introduce a few colourful flowering subjects to brighten plant displays.

Early in the year hydrangeas and *azaleas indica* are probably the most popular, and on Mothering Sunday there seems little doubt that the reasonably priced saintpaulia is the flowering plant with most appeal.

Hydrangeas Hydrangeas are best bought when flowers are coloured but not too far out. To prolong their indoor life a light position in a cool room is advised, and they will need plenty of water and frequent feeding. Plants can be kept in pots for flowering in subsequent years, but it is usually better to plant them in the garden when they are no longer attractive indoors. The ground into which they are to be planted out of doors should be well watered, and so should the plant itself.

Azaleas Azaleas also need a cool, light room in order that their flower life should be prolonged, and rain water is best for watering; never allow the plants to dry out. After flowering, when there is no longer any risk of frost, about mid-May, azaleas can be put out in the garden in either a sunny or shaded position. It is best to dig a shallow trench and fill it with moist peat into which the pot is then plunged up to

33

its rim. During the summer keep the compost wet and spray the foliage over regularly. About mid-September the plant is taken indoors again to a light, cool room and kept moist until flower buds appear. Warmer conditions are then needed for a brief spell until the flowers actually open after which the plants can be returned to cooler conditions.

Forcing plants into flower in heated greenhouses often upsets their flowering rhythm for the following year, so the first season after purchase the number of flowers produced may be disappointing. However, if one is patient and can tolerate keeping the plant over the first season without flowers subsequent years can be very rewarding. Potting-on is needed only every second or third year, when a mixture composed entirely of peat and leafmould is best.

Saintpaulias The saintpaulias can be the most trying or the most rewarding of indoor plants, depending on how one gets on with them. My experience suggests that the kitchen windowsill is one of the best places for growing them if specialised conditions cannot be provided. Most kitchen windowsills offer ample light, frequent changes of air and the warm, moist conditions which are ideal for African Violets.

Ample light is important—about twelve hours each day is necessary. It can be either artificial or natural light, or a mixture of both. Keep the compost moist and when watering be particularly careful not to get any water on the flowers or leaves; this is especially important if the plants are in a sunny window. Remove dead flowers and leaves as they appear, and for best results maintain a temperature in the region of 66°F (18°C).

Saintpaulias that are reluctant to flower, though producing lots of leaves, probably need a change of fertiliser—something with a greater amount of potash in its composition.

Aphelandra brockfeld

Spring and Summer Plants In Spring, there are calceolarias and cinnerarias in abundance, both of which need standard house plant culture to keep them in good order. After flowering the dustbin is the best place for them!

Gloxinias, fuchsias and aphelandras are available in summer. The gloxinia needs more or less the same conditions and treatment as the saintpaulia, but needs very careful handling, as the leaves are extremely brittle and break off at a touch.

Fuchsias grown indoors are rather disappointing as the flowers and buds drop off for no apparent reason although healthy when bought. This is due mainly to a change in conditions, and in particular to a change in the amount of light to which the plant has become accustomed. Radical changes in temperature and the amount of water will also cause flowers to drop. Yet, in a light greenhouse, conservatory, or even in the garden, there is no more rewarding plant than this one. In the greenhouse we can have a positive abundance of flowers from March through to October if watering, feeding and potting-on (annually) is not neglected.

Aphelandra brockfeld is normally sold with a care card

attached indicating that it is a difficult plant to manage. To many would-be purchasers this can be off-putting, which is a pity as I have found the plant easier to care for indoors than the delicate tag suggests. The most important factors are to ensure that the compost never dries out and that there is plenty of light (not necessarily direct sunlight), and that fertiliser is given regularly. It is very important to give this regular dose of fertiliser, as the aphelandra produces such a mass of roots that fertilisers can be applied at double the manufacturer's recommended strength and no harm will be done. After flowering, the plant should be cut back to a good pair of leaves and fresh growth will later develop from the axils of these leaves. A slightly heavier compost is required when potting aphelandras, so use John Innes No. 3 and pot a little more firmly than recommended for general indoor plants.

Cyclamen Later in the year we again have azaleas, cyclamen and poinsettias, and the last of these has become by far the most popular flowering plant for Christmas decoration.

Cyclamen and central heating do not go well together, as it is particularly important that the plant should enjoy cool, light and airy conditions. A maximum temperature of 55°F

(*Left*) Monstera deliciosa; (*right*) Poinsettia

(14°C) is ample; any higher and the plant will almost certainly produce yellow leaves, and its life indoors be considerably reduced. Buy plants with a few flowers fully open and plenty of buds to follow; the same advice applies when buying azaleas.

After flowering the cyclamen will quite naturally begin to die back; as leaves begin to yellow the amount of water is gradually reduced until the compost is quite dry. The pot with its corm should then be put out in the garden or under the greenhouse staging (if one is available) and kept dry until growth begins to develop in the centre of the corm. Watering can then recommence, or at this time all the old compost can be removed and the corm can be potted up in the same pot in a fresh mixture.

Poinsettias Poinsettias need a temperature of at least 60°F (16°C) a light position and weekly feeding with a liquid fertiliser from the time of purchase until the leaves begin to yellow and drop off. It is impossible to give a definite time for dying down of leaves, as some plants shed them quickly while others take several months, depending on cultivation. When plants have shed their leaves and bracts (deeply coloured leaves surrounding the tiny flowers at the top of a plant) and have lost their attraction, the stems of the plant should be cut back to some four inches from the top of the pot. The compost should then be kept just moist and the plant is stored in a warm room where the temperature does not fall below 50°F (10°C). Under normal conditions the cutting back operation is performed about mid-March and the plant is then kept dry for six to eight weeks until such time as new growth appears; when growth is evident watering should be restarted.

At a temperature of about 68°F (18°C) in a light, sunny window poinsettias will grow quite rapidly. When a reasonable number of leaves have been produced plants can be potted on, using J. I. No. 2 compost. Vigorous plants can have their growing tips removed when they have attained a height of some six to eight inches.

Poinsettias flower naturally in late November/December, but can be induced to flower at other times by controlling the amount of light they receive. This is done in commercial establishments by blacking out greenhouses with black polythene. However, the process can work in reverse indoors. Then if plants are subjected to more than the normal length of daylight from October onwards, they will continue to produce green leaves and fail to develop coloured bracts. It is therefore important to ensure that from late September until bracts appear that the plants are exposed only to normal daylight, as any additional artificial light in the evening will prevent coloured bracts from appearing. Plants can either be kept in a room used only during the day, or moved to an unlit room in the evening, or covered over in order to protect them against the artificial light.

There are so many other flowering plants available during the course of the year that it would be impossible to mention them all here. But, whatever the plant, the indoor cultivation is very similar—a light airy room, moderate temperature, water and fertiliser as recommended. They will then give a deal of pleasure.

POT–ET–FLEUR

This is a decoration consisting of growing plants, in or out of pots, arranged in a group with cut flowers. It is particularly attractive as it combines the sculptural beauty of foliage with the colour impact of cut flowers. The plants act as a background or setting for the flowers. A pot-et-fleur is both economical and time-saving as the plants are a permanent decoration with the cut flowers added when desired and available. It is also economical in that it requires so few flowers. Plants are gregarious like most people, and are often

A pot-et-fleur in a Victorian wash-bowl

happier grouped together than living alone. In the winter when foliage is scarce and arrangements of shop flowers look rather bare, the plants provide the missing foliage.

WITH PLANTS OUT OF POTS

Containers The essential function of a container is to allow the plants to be watered without the water overflowing. It must also be deep enough for the largest plant to be 1 in. below its rim when planted, and wide enough to give room for the roots of all the plants to spread out.

The container should fit in with its surroundings. Simple modern versions suit modern homes and sculptural plants, whilst period and traditional backgrounds need the older type. There are some containers—the 'classics', as it were—that harmonise with all environments. Very shiny or decorative pots should be avoided if possible, as they can detract from the beauty of the plants and flowers.

39

Removing a plant from its pot

Method Place a layer of gravel or broken crocks in the bottom of the container for good drainage. Then fill the container loosely with John Innes compost No. 2. A little charcoal added to this keeps water from going stale. Remove each plant from its pot. This is done by spreading the palm of the hand over the top of the pot, holding the plant stem between the fingers. Turn the pot upside down and rap the edge sharply against something hard. The plant should then drop into the hand. This happens more easily if the plant has not just been watered, and squeezing plastic pots is usually enough to loosen the ball of soil. Place the plant, complete with root ball, on to the compost and arrange the other plants similarly. It is wise not to firm into the compost until you are happy with the artistic grouping. Having tried all the plants in position, then firm in so that the level is about 1″ below the rim of the container, to allow for watering. Plants do not like disturbance and this is the reason for arranging the whole group before firming in. It is not necessary to put each plant absolutely upright and pleasing effects can be made when a few plants are placed at an angle. When planting, leave a small space in the centre or at the side for a receptacle for cut flowers.

Choice of Plants for Conditions Choose plants for grouping together that like the same degrees of light, heat and humidity.

MAKING A POT-ET-FLEUR
(*left to right*) A layer of gravel; plants placed in compost; cut flowers added

A plant that likes shade will be miserable with a group that prefers light, and will soon die.

The plants chosen should also like the same amount of water. It is possible, however, to keep a plant drier than its companions by wrapping its roots in polythene before planting. This keeps the moisture out and is a particularly useful device with sansevieria, a plant that likes less water than many but is valuable, because of its height, in a pot-et-fleur.

Care should be taken in the choice of plants so that they provide contrast of form and texture. It is only too easy to achieve an indeterminate mass of greenery, but variety and interest come only with practice.

For instance, a plant with fussy small foliage needs one with plain large leaves next to it, and small plants look attractive nestling in the front with taller plants behind. Pendulous plants such as hederas, chlorophytum and ivy-leaved geranium soften the hard outline of the container if they are encouraged to droop over its rim, and the heavy, wide impression a pot-

41

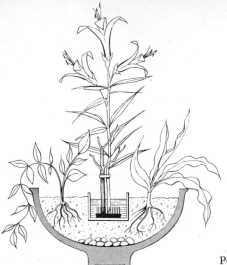

Pot-et-fleur construction

et-fleur is liable to make can be lessened by using a tall plant —palm, aspidistra, dracaena or sansevieria—in the centre. Alternatively, cut flowers can be used to add height to the design.

Colour of plants Since colour can be introduced with the cut flowers it is less important than form and texture in the choice of plants, however, the effect even then can be un-interesting unless different tints and shades of, for instance, green are used. A pale green plant looks better next to a dark green one, and variegated foliage is useful. Each plant should be clearly seen amongst its neighbours, and all will be individually appreciated where there is variety and contrast of form, texture and colour. The plants tend to arrange themselves as they search for light and space and the pot-et-fleur settles down and looks better after two or three weeks.

The Flowers These can be added when available although the plants can sit happily on their own if well arranged. Flowers of the different seasons can give surprisingly different effects

when used with the same plants. For example spring daffodils give quite a different appearance from autumn chrysanthemums. Bold, dramatic and large flowers look the most
effective, while little fussy flowers look out of scale and
become lost. Good effects are obtained with lilies of all kinds,
arums in particular, daffodils, tulips, iris, peonies and orchids.
Round shaped rather than spiky flowers are usually better.

The Flower Container The easiest container to use is a small
meat tin painted with black emulsion paint so that it 'vanishes'.
It should be deep enough to hold enough water for the flowers
and wide enough to hold a pinholder (see chapter four) to
support the stems. Ease the tin into the compost, fill with
water and add the flowers. The flowers should be slightly
turned in different directions so that they do not all face the
same way. If the container for the complete pot-et-fleur is
deep rather than wide, an empty cigar tube can be plunged
into the compost and flowers put into this.

For special occasions a very big plant looks dramatic with
flowers added. Metal cones, 4"–6" long, which hold water
are sold by florists. These can be taped to the stem of the
plant at different heights to hold the flowers.

Driftwood, Shells, Coral, Stones These fit naturally into a
pot-et-fleur. Driftwood can give height and a change of
texture as well as providing support for climbing plants.
Small pieces of wood can be placed in the front of the flower
containers to hide them, a purpose for which shells, coral and
stones can also be used.

WITH PLANTS IN POTS

The plants can be left in their own pots. This has two
great advantages—the plant can easily be removed from the
pot-et-fleur or re-positioned without disturbing the other
plants, and plants with differing water requirements can be

grouped together. The great *dis*advantage is the amount of room taken up by the pots, which means a very large container. This gives a heavy look which can sometimes be counteracted by using a tall plant.

Method Place gravel in the bottom of the container. Add the pots of plants and then cover all the pots with moist peat. This gives a high humidity which the plants enjoy. Moss can be used as an alternative to peat or to cover the peat.

Flowers Cut flowers can be added in receptacles of water as above.

OTHER IDEAS

At Christmas time, artificial poinsettias or Christmas roses can be added instead of fresh flowers.

Various fresh edible fruits can be arranged in a bowl and a pot plant added, so hiding the pot with the fruit, or else the plant can be taken out and put into a polythene bag. Flowers can be added to fruit in a tube or small container.

Spring bulbs seem to take a long time to come into flower even after they are brought into the house. A plant put into the centre of the bowl gives interest until the bulbs come into flower and room should be left for this at the time of planting the bulbs. Alternatively a few cut flowers can be added in a small container.

A piece of driftwood on a base can have plants in polythene bags tucked around it to make an interesting decoration.

CARE OF POT–ET–FLEUR

The usual care (as described in chapter one) is all that is needed. Watering and feeding is also as usual. The flower container may be small and need topping up with water which is quickly used up. Fresh plants should replace those which die or deteriorate.

3

Cut and Keep

Flowers are so incredibly beautiful that few of us can resist them, but many people hesitate to put cut flowers in their homes as they feel they may quickly wilt and that they are an expensive short-lived luxury. This can be true. However, knowing how to cut, buy and prepare flowers for the house means a much longer life for them, and knowing something about their display and arrangement often means that fewer need be bought. It is also possible to make large arrangements with only one or two flowers by "stretching" them with other compatible material so that the cost is minimal.

A flower's life is short because having spilled its pollen and fulfilled its basic function by beginning a new generation, its work is over. Nothing then prevents it fading. But there is a difference between dying and wilting and many flowers are thrown away not because they are over but because they have wilted. A little time spent in selection and preparation can prevent wilt and sometimes prolong the life of a flower too.

BOUGHT FLOWERS

There are excellent flower shops now and people buy flowers for many reasons: because they have no gardens, because of winter, because they prefer not to pick their own flowers or for more and better variety.

It is wise to know something about the signs which mean

that a flower is fresh, although few florists knowingly sell poor flowers.

Whenever possible, buy in bud. You can then watch and enjoy the buds unfurling into beautiful flowers in your own home. A wide open flower gives less time for enjoyment before it fades. Many growers now send flowers to market in tight bud, in particular narcissus, daffodils, irises, tulips, lilies, roses, gladioli.

Signs of Age Where you can, look at the centres of flowers— young ones have light yellow centres, older ones are a darker gold. A lot of loose pollen means the flower is mature and nearing the end of its life. Chrysanthemums and carnations should have tightly curled petals at the centre. Chrysanthemums often have a dimple in the centre, a depression in the petals. Neither should have drooping or dropping petals at the outside edges. Scabious should have a light green centre. If it is fluffy it is too mature to buy.

Foliage should be crisp, bright in colour and not brown. If the leaves are flagging they only require a drink. Stems should not be slimy or brown stained.

Cutting Stems Once home unwrap the flowers immediately even before making your own cup of tea. Cut about $\frac{1}{2}''$ off the end of the stems. This prevents a possible airlock, which can stop water from entering the stems. Airlocks often appear when flowers are carried home and the stems become dry at the ends. Cut on the slant so that the stems have a greater area for the absorption of water. Carnations should be cut above the 'knob' as this may stop water from being absorbed. Spring flowers should have the white part of the stem removed for the same reason.

Put the flowers straight into a bucketful of tepid water until you are ready to arrange them, leaving the bucket in the coolest place you can find away from draughts and strong sunlight.

Garden flowers need a little more attention than shop flowers as the florist has probably prepared these flowers for you and had them in water for a while.

Cutting It is best to cut early in the morning or late in the evening when the plants are full of moisture. In the middle of the day the sun draws much moisture from the plant and it is more likely to wilt if cut at this time.

Cut with flower scissors, flower cutters or a knife, on a slant. A flat flower basket is useful for gathering flowers— and looks romantic. However, a bucket containing 2″–3″ water is better for the flowers because putting them immediately into water often stops a bubble of air from clogging the stem and preventing water from entering.

Cut flowers when they are in bud, but not in such tight bud that no colour can be seen, as a very green bud may have difficulty in taking up water and may never open.

Conditioning This word means filling the stem with water so that it becomes more rigid. When a flower wilts it is because there is not enough water in the stem to hold the flower erect. When flowers and foliage are cut from a plant, the source of water is removed. This source must be replaced by putting the stem end in a container of water. In a dry room, especially one with central heating, water evaporates from the flowers and foliage even more quickly than usual. As a result wilting often occurs since the water from the container is not travelling up the stem fast enough to counteract this loss of moisture. The walls of the cells then collapse. By conditioning, or filling the stem up very well with water before the flowers are arranged, this wilting can often be avoided. It takes only a short time to condition flowers and foliage and it is well worth the small amount of trouble. The methods are easy to remember as they follow the type of stem.

Stem Types

Generally speaking, stems fall into four groups:
1. Soft stems such as those of daffodils and many perennials.
2. Hard and sometimes woody stems such as those of roses, lilac and cherry blossom.
3. Hollow stems such as those of lupins and delphiniums.
4. Milky stems such as those of poppies and the euphorbias, including the red poinsettia seen at Christmas.

Treatment

1. *Soft Stems* Cut $\frac{1}{2}$" off the end of the stem and put immediately into a bucket of deep, tepid water.
2. *Hard and Woody Stems* Split the end of the stem with a knife or flower cutters for 1"–2" along the length, to make a water channel. If the stem is very thick make more than one cut. Place in a bucket of deep, tepid water.

   If the stem is also woody and has thickish bark, scrape or peel this off for 1"–2".

   Both these processes should be repeated if the stem is cut again when arranging the flowers.

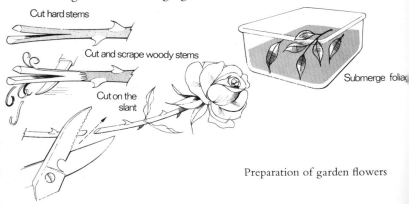

Cut hard stems

Cut and scrape woody stems

Cut on the slant

Submerge foliage

Preparation of garden flowers

STEM TREATMENT
(left) Filling a hollow stem; *(right)* Burning a milky stem

Some people prefer to hammer woody stems. This is not entirely necessary for the flower, as cutting and scraping is equally good; however it may relieve the arranger's frustrations and prevent him or her knocking their beloved on the head.

3. *Hollow Stems* Hold upside down and fill with water by means of a narrow spouted watering can. Plug the stem end with a piece of cotton wool or alternatively hold your thumb over the end until you have placed the stem in a bucket of deep tepid water. If the stem has to be cut again, cut under water and then hold the thumb over the end when the stem is removed from the water.

4. *Milky Stems* The ends of these should be burnt with a candle flame, a match or the flame of a gas jet. Hold the stem in the flame until it blackens and stops sizzling. This stops the milky fluid from running out. Place the stem in deep, tepid water. If the stem is cut again when arranging the flowers, this process should be repeated.

49

FOLIAGE

Foliage should be *submerged* in a bowl or sink of water because a leaf can take in water through its surface tissue without spoiling. Grey foliage is the only exception when submerging should be avoided as it causes loss of greyness. Long branches can be submerged in the bath, family permitting.

These methods are really very quick and do not take as long to do as to describe.

When flowers and foliage are all prepared and in water, put them in a cool, draughtless place, out of strong light for at least two hours. Flowers picked in the evening can be left overnight. After a minimum of two hours they should be full of water and ready to arrange and enjoy.

WILTED FLOWERS

Sometimes a flower does not respond to the normal treatment. In this case first aid treatment is necessary and there are three methods.

1. Cut an inch off the end of the stem under water and leave the flower in deep water for two hours. This may do the trick by removing a possible airlock.

2. Float the flower on water for about two hours. This is often a successful method to use for wilted roses.

3. For 'shock' treatment place $\frac{1}{2}''$ of the end of the stem into a jug of very hot water while you count to 20. This expands the cell walls, forces out air bubbles and causes water to shoot up the stem. Then fill the jug with cold water and leave for two hours. This treatment really works wonders. It is wise to protect the flower heads from the steam with a towel placed over the top of the jug or by wrapping the flower heads in tissue paper or a polythene bag. This hot water treatment is also good for any flowers which seem difficult to condition by normal methods. It can be done when the flower is first cut from

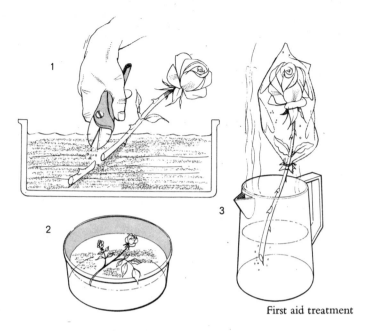

First aid treatment

the garden, and I *always* do it with garden roses. The hot water will cause the end of some stems to become floppy. this needs to be cut off before arranging the flower.

ADDITIVES

There are many old wives tales about extending the life of a flower by adding things to the water in the container, such as a penny, aspirin, sugar, vinegar. When I was once spraying arrangements in Chester Cathedral to keep them fresh for a flower festival, one dear old lady asked me if I was giving them gin. Some of these, and possibly gin, do have slight value for certain flowers, but experiments have proved that the difference they make is hardly worth the trouble in our busy lives. However special treatment for certain flowers is listed later.

One additive has been found very worthwhile. From experiments in hospitals it was found that many good woman-hours were being lost when nurses changed the water in flower containers daily to avoid bacteria. If $\frac{1}{4}$ teaspoon chlorhexidine is added to each pint of water at the time of first putting the flowers in water, this mild disinfectant will discourage the growth of bacteria for as long as two weeks. This means that flowers need not be disturbed for water changing, something they anyhow dislike, and much time is saved.

ARRANGING THE FLOWERS

While the flowers are conditioning, choose a suitable container. This should be clean in order to discourage the growth of bacteria. Also choose a method of supporting the flowers to suit the container. The methods of support are called 'mechanics' and are described in chapter four.

Add some disinfected water to the container before you start arranging. Then take the flowers one by one straight from the bucket and arrange them in the container, or alternatively it will not hurt to put them on a piece of polythene beside the container, as long as they are not left out of water for too long. Always strip off any foliage which would be below water as this would become slimy and cause bacteria to form.

Many people find it helps to arrange the flowers in the place where they are to be displayed, so that the size and shape of the design will fit the surroundings. A piece of polythene on the furniture and under the container prevents damage. Another piece on the floor prevents the carpet getting wet.

After arranging the flowers top up the container with water. By placing a finger just over the rim of the container you can feel when the water is reaching the top and so prevent a flood. The container may need topping up every day as water is absorbed quickly by plant material and also evaporates in a dry room. Changing the water is not necessary if chlorhexidine has been added.

The best position in a room for long-lasting flowers is out of sunshine or strong light, away from radiators or central heating grilles and out of the way of draughts. In very cold weather putting them on a windowsill is a mistake as the flowers can be damaged by frost when the curtains are drawn.

SPECIAL TREATMENT

Carnations Cut just above a knuckle. 1 level teaspoon of sugar to 1 pint of water can lengthen the life of a flower for up to 2 days.

Clematis Immerse the whole flower in water for about 1 hour.

Clematis vitalba (Old Man's Beard) lasts well in a mixture of 1 part of glycerine to 2 parts of water.

Acacia (mimosa wattle) should be kept in a polythene bag until the last minute before arranging. Spraying with water once arranged also helps to retard drying out which happens very quickly.

Anemones and the narcissus family are not happy in water retaining plastic foam.

Bulbous plants should be arranged in shallow water after the first conditioning in deep water or the stems can become soggy and not rigid.

Tulips, arum leaves, ferns, acanthus benefit from starch water instead of plain water. It helps to keep them stiff. The recipe is 2 teaspoons of instant starch to $1\frac{1}{2}$ pints of water.

Violets drink well through their petals and should be upturned in a saucer of water every day.

Hydrangea The flower heads should be immersed in water for a minimum of one hour, but not longer than overnight, as the petals may become transparent.

Ranunculus should be wrapped tightly in newspaper while conditioning to keep the stems stiff. This is also helpful with tulips.

Gerberas last well if they are given the hot water treatment at once, as for wilted flowers.

Bulrushes can be sprayed with hair lacquer to prevent them blowing. Hair lacquer sprayed on the backs of geraniums and lupins can stop the petals dropping for a while.

Lilac and also philadelphus, viburnum opulus (guelder rose) Remove all the foliage because it takes moisture away from the flowers, and place 4″ of the scraped and split stem in very hot water for 30 minutes.

Lilies The pollen can stain both the flower and your clothing badly. The anthers may be cut off to prevent this.

Hellebore (Christmas rose) These are tricky to condition but will last very well when picked in the fruit stage.

Holly Berries The birds can take these well before Christmas. If you pick them early to avoid this put the stems in a bucket half full of water with a polythene bag over the top, tucked into the bucket. The berries stay surprisingly fresh.

RETARDING FLOWERS

It is possible to retard flowers in the refrigerator. The perfect temperature is 5.5°C. Seal the flowers in foil or polythene after an initial soak. Roses, carnations, tulips and lilac can be held back in this way for a week should you want to keep them for a special occasion. Peonies and gladioli can be left on a cold stone floor out of water for a few days. When you want to use them, cut the stems and place in deep warm water to condition as usual.

FORCING BRANCHES

Branches can be persuaded to open in the house to produce early flowers in the spring. Suitable plants are forsythia, witchhazel, magnolia, cherry, almond, crab, pear, plum, apple. Cut branches which have a sign of life about them and large buds. Immerse the whole branch in a bath of hot water (the heat the hand can stand and no hotter) for 4–5 hours. This warms the sap and softens the husks of the buds. After submerging split the stems for an inch or two, scrape off the outer bark of the same two inches and put the branches into lukewarm water in a light place. You can then watch the buds gradually unfurl.

TRANSPORTING PLANT MATERIAL

Florists' Flowers should be carefully wrapped so that the heads are protected. The cool winds or hot sun of the street and the draughts of the Underground are all harmful to flowers.

Countryside Flowers and Foliage should be put into polythene bags and tied up. If possible dip them in a stream first and keep out of the sun, especially in the polythene bag. The bag with full sun on it becomes a 'hothouse' and the flowers develop too quickly.

Garden Flowers can also be packed in polythene bags. Even if the bag is only placed over the stem, moisture is retained. In very hot weather a cardboard box with a few airholes in it is preferable to polythene. The flowers should just be laid in the box *without* absorbent paper or sheets of polythene. When packing you will find that the flowers themselves are the best support for each other. They should be placed so that flower heads are not on top of one another.

4

Practical Points

It is a great help to have the right tools and supports for arranging flowers and there is no need for them to cost a lot of money. These things make all the difference to the arrangement of flowers and avoid frustration, wasted time and effort.

TOOLS

Flower Cutters The first essential is a pair of flower cutters. The flower scissors sold by florists are inexpensive and also cut light wire. A pair of secateurs is also necessary for thick, woody stems. A more expensive but well worthwhile pair of cutters does both jobs—cuts all wire and thick stems as well. They are compact and easy to handle.

Watering Can The type with a long curved spout is useful for reaching into the smallest aperture in containers and for watering plants.

Buckets Tall buckets with a handle on each side are made especially for flowers and can be obtained from florists.

MECHANICS

This is a collective term meaning the supports used for holding plant material in place and refers to pinholders, wire netting, water-retaining plastic foam, stub and reel wire, cocktail sticks, cones, candlecups.

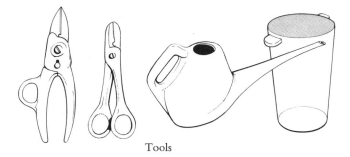

Tools

Pinholders These are heavy round or oblong lead bases in various sizes from $\frac{1}{2}''$ to $5''$ in diameter. Into the lead are fixed a series of small vertical pins. The ends are sharp and point upwards. Do tell any friend to whom you give one as a present that it is not a tool for combing the dog or pricking pastry, as they do seem rather odd looking objects until you see how accurately they hold flower stems in position. The sharp pins impale any stems pressed on to them with the exception of very slender stems which slip between the pins and have to be supported by other means. Pinholders are called 'kenzans' in Japan and 'frogs' and needlepoint holders in America. Flower shops and big stores sell them.

The heaviest and most expensive are the best and most economical buy in the long run. It is advisable to buy several of $2''$ or more diameter. The small ones are difficult to handle, hold only a few stems and are more useful for specialised work rather than normal flower arranging. The heaviest kind are the best because they do not slip in the container.

Look at the pins when buying to make sure they are *close* together.

When using a pinholder push the flower stem firmly on but be careful of your fingers. The stem is held upright. If you want to angle a stem, press gently down to one side *after* you have pushed the stem straight down on the pinholder,

57

Pinholders built into a metal dish are very useful. They are called well-type pinholders and can be used when a container does not hold water or on a flat piece of wood, covered cake board or any type of base (see chapter five), without any other container being necessary. Well-pinholders do not hold much water so are not good for thirsty flowers or for a large quantity. They are excellent for spring bulbous flowers which like shallow water. Some arrangers make their own well-type pinholder by putting a normal pinholder into a small tin. Make sure, if you do this, that the tin is higher than the pins so that water can reach the stem ends. If the tin is painted with a dark emulsion paint it will not show.

Another type of pinholder has only a few pins which are wide apart. They are for holding blocks of water-retaining plastic material in position and are equally useful. There is also a very inexpensive plastic one.

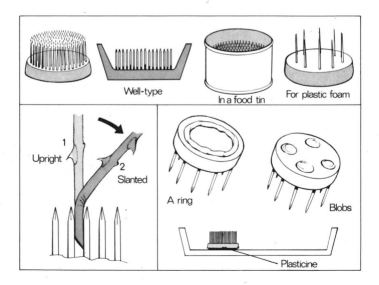

Well-type

In a food tin

For plastic foam

1
Upright

2
Slanted

A ring

Blobs

Plasticine

(*Top*) Pin holders (*left*) Impaling a stem (*Right*) Plasticine

Pinholders are normally used for simple arrangements and particularly in shallow containers. When a larger quantity of plant material is used in one design, a second support in addition to the pinholder is often necessary. This is described later under 'wire netting'.

Many pinholders are heavy enough to stay in position in the container, but for extra safety place a ring of plasticine on the base of the pinholder. Press on firmly. Four small blobs of plasticine placed at even intervals may be used instead. Press the pinholder firmly down on to the container and give a small twist. It is essential that both pinholder, plasticine and container are absolutely dry or the plasticine will not stick. Sealing Strip can also be used.

Wire Netting A very inexpensive method of support for stems is wire netting or chicken wire from the ironmonger. This is useful to have in three sizes of mesh—2″, 1″ and ½″. The 2″ mesh is used for the larger and deeper type of container and the 1″ and ½″ mesh for using with plastic foam, described later.

Cut the mesh as wide as the container and roughly three times its depth. Remove the thick selvedge. Bend into a 'U'. Squeeze or crumple it so that the cut ends are at the top and push well down into the container, filling the space with the crumpled netting. It should not be so tight that stems cannot be inserted and the cut ends should stick up above the rim of the container. These can then be used for winding around stems to hold them in position.

It is wise to secure the netting to the container so that it does not slip about. This can be done by sliding an elastic band around the whole thing—container and wire netting, or with wire from a reel sold by florists and ironmongers. A small piece of this wire can be used to secure the netting to the handles or rim of the container or a larger piece can be taken around the container and secured to the mesh on the

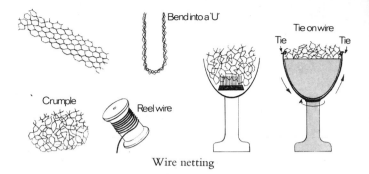

Bend into a 'U'

Crumple

Reel wire

Tie on wire

Tie   Tie

Wire netting

opposite side. Large containers require two pieces of wire to be carried round the container and secured in this way at right angles. Wire netting is best used in conjunction with a pinholder so that the heavy stems are impaled at the ends and also supported by the netting higher up. Lighter stems can be simply pushed into the netting without impaling the end on the pinholder. The wire netting and pinholder method of support is best for deep containers and large arrangements. Arrangements on pedestals perhaps 7' high use this method of support.

The use of the smaller mesh is explained later.

Cones or Tubes Sometimes long-stemmed plant material is not available just when you need it for a tall arrangement. Special cones or tubes can be bought at the florist or an empty cigar case or orchid tube can be used to lengthen short stems. The cone should be attached to a garden stick at the height you require with wire or sellotape. Push the stick through the wire netting and impale it on the pinholder. Fill the cone with water and a little wire netting on water retaining plastic foam. You then have a raised device, holding water, into which a stem can be inserted at a greater height than would otherwise be possible. It is best not to use a cone unless really necessary as the result can look contrived and

60

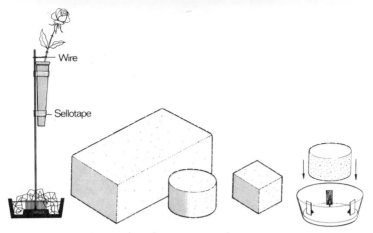

Using a tube, Plastic Foam and a Foam Saucer

the cone difficult to hide. Painting with matt black paint helps to conceal it. The cones should be used for plant material which is normally long-stemmed, such as delphiniums. A primrose in a cone at the top of a large arrangement looks very much out of place.

Foamed Plastic This is a very light material which can be quickly filled with water. It makes flower arrangement simple because a stem pushed into it stays in position at *any* angle. This means that containers which do not hold water can be used and that unusual effects and styles can be accomplished. It is particularly good for low arrangements on dining tables. Its disadvantages are that it is more expensive than wire netting, it cannot be used indefinitely and some flowers do not last in it as long as they do in water.

The foam is green and sold in several sizes by florists. It can be cut easily with a knife to fit the size of a container. It is advisable to leave some of it above the edge of the container for downward flowing stems.

It must be soaked before use, by placing in a receptacle of water which is *deeper* than the block of foam. It is ready to use when the block drops in the water and is almost level with the surface. Small rounds take about ten minutes and larger blocks take twenty minutes to soak up enough water. The large blocks should be soaked *horizontally*. They weigh 2 oz. before soaking and 4 lb. afterwards, which just shows how much water is retained. No more water is absorbed by leaving the foam to soak longer than 20 minutes.

After soaking, place in the container. If possible leave room at the sides for further water. The foam does dry out and so it is best used standing in water. It is also helpful to pour a little water on to it every day. Once dried out it is not possible to wet it again. Spare wet foam should be kept in a polythene bag. One friend was delighted by his wife's interest in flower arrangement until he found wet plastic foam in his bed.

Containers which do not hold water should have the foam wrapped in a polythene bag which prevents the loss of moisture. The stems of the plant material are then pushed through the polythene into the foam. This is not recommended for everyday use as it is difficult to push the stems through the polythene and a sharp skewer may be needed to make holes for the stems.

Florists also sell inexpensive plastic saucers, or holders, for the blocks of foam. These are for use in place of a container and are excellent for taking to hospitals, for table arrangements where the container is hidden, or for use on a base, such as a slice of wood. Hospital nurses are delighted when flowers arrive already arranged.

It is sometimes helpful to use a 'cap' of wire netting over a block of foam. This gives a second support if the foam should start to crumble through constant use. It is also helpful for very heavy stems which might swing in the foam. $1''$ mesh for normal stems and $\frac{1}{2}''$ mesh for small stems is the best. The wire netting is *not* crumpled in this case but is used flat on top of the foam. Cut a piece which fits over the top and down the sides and press the netting gently over the foam. If the

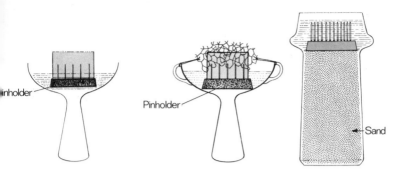

inholder

Pinholder

Sand

(*Left*) Plastic foam in a pinholder; (*Centre*) with wire netting; (*Right*) Pinholder with sand in a container

container has handles or anything else to which wire can be attached secure the netting to the handles with a short length of florists' reel wire. If there is no way to attach the wire, then an elastic band or Sellotape can be put round foam, netting and container until the arrangement is finished. Then it can be cut off if it shows.

The pinholders made specially for use with the foam, with pins wide apart are excellent stabilisers. They are heavy and hold the foam in position firmly.

Sand Very tall containers can be a problem. Wire netting disappears into them and can become a rusty muddle. Pinholders on the bottom mean a great waste of stem and only long stems can be used. Try filling the container $\frac{3}{4}$ full with wet sand and place a pinholder or wire netting or both on top of the sand. You can now work much higher up. Providing the sand is wet you can continue to pour water into the container and the top $\frac{1}{4}$ will be full of clear water for the plant material to stand in.

Candlecups These are metal or plastic saucers with small knobs underneath which fit into a candlestick or a bottle with a narrow neck. These candlecups hold a pinholder or plastic foam and wire netting, whichever is more suitable. Concealing candlecups is often difficult and the amount of plant material required to do this often gives a top-heavy appearance. In a candlestick they are often wobbly, unless plasticine is used to hold them in place. Bottles often look better without a candlecup. In this case the arrangement is gathered together in the hand. A piece of wire is wound around the stems and the whole arrangement is dropped straight into the neck of the container.

Cocktail Sticks These are invaluable for holding fruit in position and do not spoil the fruit like wire. Press half of a stick into one piece of fruit and the other half into another. Neither will then roll about. Fruit can be secured in grouped heaps in this way and still be eaten later.

Stub Wires These are obtained at florists in various lengths and gauges. Most flowers look more natural if they are not wired, but a broken stem can be given a splint if a wire is run inside the stem. They are also useful for hyacinth whose heavy head causes the stem to flop.

Guide a wire along the inside of the stem leaving about an inch sticking out at the bottom. Push this end into the plastic foam making sure that the end of the flower stem goes into

(*Left*) Using a candlecup; (*Centre*) using a cocktail stick; (*Right*) Stub wires and wiring a hyacinth

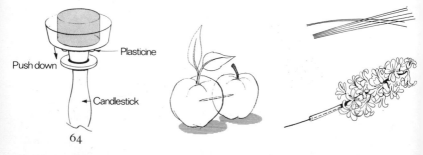

Plasticine

Push down

Candlestick

the foam a little way to receive water. The wire however acts as a support. Clivia can be similarly wired.

HIDING THE MECHANICS

None of the above mechanics is expensive or difficult to use and their use soon becomes second nature. *Beware of having larger mechanics than are needed to support the flowers.* Mechanics are not attractive to look at and should be hidden, which is difficult when they are large. Adding more and more foliage to conceal wire netting or plastic foam can result in an unnecessarily heavy looking flower arrangement and a waste of plant material.

Deep containers hide the mechanics automatically and the small amount of netting sticking above the rim is soon covered with leaves cut short and placed close to the netting.

Plastic foam can be covered with plant material cut *very short* and pushed up to the foam. Foliage is best for this. As the foam is green it soon seems to disappear.

Pinholders used alone are best for shallow containers as they can be hidden more easily than wire netting. Foliage can be used but quite often the design of the arrangement is spoilt when foliage is added at the base and to avoid this a collection of other small objects becomes very useful. Pebbles or small stones can be piled over the pinholder to hide it and often add a natural charm to the arrangement. A small piece of weathered wood, bark or coral can often be found to tuck around the pinholder. Small shells, marbles and even pieces of washed coal have their uses. Glass from a shattered windscreen looks lovely over the pinholder in a water arrangement. This can be obtained easily from the roadside but it is probably safer to ask a garage to save you the next shattered windscreen that comes in. Make sure it is the kind which does not cut your hand. By leaving our car out on a freezing night I acquired a box full of glass chunks.

This method is not popular with husbands.

5

Containers and Bases

CONTAINERS

Receptacles for flowers used to be called vases but a more general term 'containers' is now popular and this covers a much broader field. With the arrival of plastic foam it is not even necessary for the container to be capable of holding water. *Almost anything* can be used as a container but it should enhance the flowers and not vie with them for attention. Collecting containers is half the fun of flower arrangement. Almost every town has junk and antique shops, china and flower shops, perhaps markets and auction sales in which to search. I have containers from all over the world. A range is the ideal to possess as different containers suit different flowers and seasons. If you are a beginner it is wise not to buy many to start with. Your choice may differ as you learn more about flower arrangement. Invest in several good pinholders including a well-type. The latter can be used on all kinds of bases without a container.

Small containers are difficult for beginners—the mechanics are fiddly and they encourage cutting very short flower stems. An aperture of not less than 4″–5″ diameter is advisable to start with.

Colour Colour is important. Containers, except in more advanced abstract work, should play second fiddle to the flowers. In some cases containers are more suitable as features

A group of containers and figurines for flower arrangement

alone rather than as receptacles for flowers. They should enhance the flowers not vie with them for attention. If a very brilliantly coloured container is used with flowers of another colour the arrangement falls into two parts—container and flower arrangement, neither looking as though they belong to each other. The flower arrangement and container should blend together as one design. The Flemish flower paintings show this beautifully—the container never dominates or steals the picture but still remains a part of the whole design.

Brilliant colours and highly patterned containers should then be avoided. The earth's colours are always safe—brown, greys, beige, soft greens, terra cotta. The colours of metal and of modern stoneware are good. Black and white are more difficult to blend with plant material as there is no true black or white in nature's colours. White can be blended with flowers if some white plant material is used. Black is good with such things as tulips with black centres. Unfortunately most of the containers on sale seem to be black or white.

Texture The texture of a container is not so dominant as the colour but generally speaking a shiny texture detracts from the flowers, so a matt surface is safer.

Linings Containers which do not hold water can be lined with jars, tins, plastic dishes, glass bowls. The old enamel pudding bowls painted black are very useful.

Metals Copper is lovely with pink, peach, mauve, apricot, gold, red. It gives a feeling of warmth and welcome to a home.

Brass is not as warm looking as copper but suits yellow, orange, green and brown. Both copper and brass can dominate the plant material because they are very shiny, so it is important to use striking colouring and a larger amount of plant material than with a similar container of less shiny texture.

Bronze is a perfect foil for flowers, a good colour and not as shiny as brass and copper. Any colour is pleasing in bronze and many early Japanese containers were made of it. It is unfortunately expensive, but there are sometimes containers made of spelter which are similar but cheaper and lighter.

Pewter also harmonises well with flowers, particularly blues, mauves and pinks. Grey foliage is excellent with it. A pewter plate is a very good investment for many types of arrangement.

Metal containers are always valued for flower arrangement because their coolness helps flowers to last well and they are relatively unbreakable.

Silver is not as easy as other metals because it is very shiny and can detract from the flowers—but it is lovely with pink roses, especially when combined with grey foliage which harmonises with the silver colour.

Alabaster This is particularly harmonious with all flower colours, but water is not good for alabaster and it is best to line the container with a bowl to prevent water touching the surface. Alternatively, varnish painted on the inside of the container seals it quite well.

Baskets These are lovely at any time but especially in the summer. They can look cumbersome if they are over-filled and as basketry is a light material it looks better when the style of arrangement is light and airy and some of the inside of the basket is left showing. The secret is to avoid using a large block of plastic foam and to keep the stem ends tightly together, using length of stem to radiate from a tight centre in pleasing curves.

Pottery The handmade pots from small potteries are excellent and often original in style. Their matt textures and earth colours are particularly suitable for flowers and they cannot be bettered for the contemporary styles which use only a few branches and a minimum of plant material. Many dishes meant for the oven are suitable for flowers, particularly shallow green or brown ones. They are often inexpensive and can be used for both purposes.

Glass This is very beautiful but difficult to use because the mechanics show easily. A candlecup can be useful in the top of the container. Glass containers are most effective when placed against the light, especially if filled to the brim with water which also steadies the container with its weight. Sometimes they are better used as a feature with the flowers placed at the side.

Wood Few containers are made in wood but there are tea caddies or sewing boxes which can be used successfully as containers. Natural weathered wood is lovely if you are lucky and find a piece large enough to make a hollow place for a small tin to hold water or plastic foam.

Lead A sheet of lead with the sides turned up makes an excellent low container for 'water' arrangements. You can bend it into many pleasing shapes.

Fibreglass These containers are unbreakable, hold water and are light in weight. They are made in very good shapes, sometimes copies of old urns.

Pedestals and Pedestal Containers Stands on which a container can be placed to lift the level of the flowers are very effective for occasions such as weddings, when normal containers cannot be seen. Modern pedestals can be purchased in wood and metal but there are also very beautiful antique ones of marble, wood and metal to be found. The arrangements on pedestals should be in proportion to the height and look better if the plant material is also large in scale as small flowers seem insignificant. Quite often a room for a party, or a church for a wedding, is more effective decorated with one or two large pedestal arrangements than many smaller containers. The pedestals become a centre of interest and show the flowers to best advantage.

Some containers have built-in pedestals so that the flowers

Flowers in a pedestal container

are lifted. These are of course smaller than the pedestal stands on which a container can be placed. They have the advantage of giving space below the arrangement which is particularly attractive.

BASES

To prevent the polished surface of furniture from getting wet, many people place some sort of mat under the container. This is recognised as of practical help but it should also be treated as part of the whole design to add to the artistic appearance. It is called a base in flower arrangement.

Bases can be of irregular-shaped slices of tree-trunk which are polished, oiled or left natural, pieces of slate or stone, marble or glass. They can be formal Japanese or Chinese bases with or without feet, rush and bamboo mats, or up-turned wooden salad plates. One of the simplest can be made from a round tray or a cakeboard. Cut a piece of fabric (it can be a remnant), in the same shape but 2″ larger all round. Turn in the edge, turn in a further $\frac{1}{2}$″ and stitch. Leave a small opening and slot in a piece of elastic. Tighten the elastic and tie off so that the fabric can be easily slipped over the tray or cakeboard. One tray can have many 'slipovers' in different fabrics, textures and colours. They can be taken off for washing.

Quite often the flower arrangement seems to be too large for the container and to dominate it. By adding a base, visual weight is added which improves the balance of the design.

If on the other hand, the container seems too large for the flower arrangement, then adding a base only makes the flowers seem even less important than before. Some containers have built in bases and usually do not need another one added. To protect the furniture a small mat can be hidden under the container.

Bases can be used for flower arrangement without formal containers—for example, the plant material can be arranged

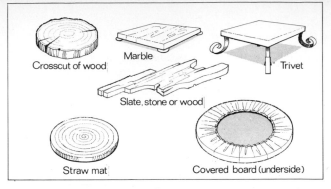

Bases

in a well-type container which is hidden by foliage and placed on a base. A stock of bases is therefore very useful and eliminates the need for so many containers.

It follows that if a base is meant to be seen it should harmonise with the other parts of the design—container and plant material. A curved base—round or oval—suits a curved container. A square or oblong base suits a similarly shaped container. Not only the shape but the style, colour and texture should be in accord with the style, colour and texture used already.

As with the container, bases should enhance and not compete with the flowers. Brilliant colours are unsuitable. Flowers are very much 'star performers' and are not happy with strong competition.

'Earth' colours, as with containers, are advisable. It is also very effective to use a greyed version or dull tone of one of the colours in the plant material. Black, grey and brown bases are usually safe and a dull or dark yellow-green is always effective as this colour is so often present in the plant material. The texture and style should also be in harmony. . For example, a slice of wood or a flat piece of stone or slate suits a design of wild flowers, preserved plant material or a landscape scene. A piece of velvet fabric is in keeping with traditional containers and basketry, rush mats or bamboo suit modern pottery.

6

Lasting Beauty

Beauty is not always in a scarlet robe,
She wears an old black shawl;
She flouts the flesh and shows the bone,
When winter trees are tall.
More beautiful than fact maybe,
The shadow on the wall.

V. Sackville West

It seems almost unbelievable that a leaf from a plant can be treated so that it lasts ten years or more, but it is quite possible. A store of preserved leaves and flowers is most useful for arrangements in winter when plant material is expensive to buy and in poor condition in the garden. It is also useful at all times for people without gardens. Preserved plant material can be mixed with fresh flowers or leaves, or it can be used by itself and left unchanged for several weeks, to save time. Just as fruit is bottled and jammed in the summer to have in winter when there is little variety in food, summer flowers and foliage can be preserved for decoration.

PRESERVING WITH GLYCERINE

This is the best method of all. The results are long-lasting, easy to handle and store, the plant material does not shrink as in drying but is pliable and strong and the colours are rich, mostly shades of brown. It is not possible to keep the green

73

colour. Glycerine preserves foliage so that it never needs to be put in water again.

Recipe Mix together one part of glycerine to two parts of water. If the water is very hot the two will mix together more quickly. Some chemists sell rough glycerine which is cheaper than the refined type. A bottle containing 250 ml. is enough for average use. Pour the glycerine into a narrow jar and fill the bottle twice over with the hot water. This washes out all the glycerine. *Stir well with a spoon.* This is important otherwise the glycerine stays at the bottom and the results are not good. Branches of leaves or if necessary single leaves are then stood in the mixture. It does not matter if it is still warm. Before putting in hard and woody stems split and scrape them, as in conditioning. Remove poor leaves beforehand as it is a waste to glycerine damaged foliage. Stand the jar in a dry place as the plant material can mildew in a damp atmosphere. The glycerine should always reach about 1″–2″ up the stem. If the mixture runs out before the leaves are preserved, add some more.

Timing The plant material is preserved when it has completely changed colour. Often you can see the brown colour creeping up the leaves. The time varies according to the type of plant and is given below. If the foliage is left too long beads of glycerine will appear and should be wiped off as they can make greasy marks on such things as wallpaper. When preserved, store in a box in a dry place. The glycerine mixture can be used again and again. A quarter teaspoonful of chlorhexidine to 1 pint of glycerine and water prevents mould occurring in the mixture.

Plant Material There are many plants which preserve well with glycerine and a few which will not take it at all. A list of the best plants is given later. It is interesting however to keep a permanent jar of the mixture going and to add different plants at different times of the year.

When to Cut As a general rule glycerine is best absorbed when the leaves are middle-aged. Young foliage does not take it well and old foliage is not taking up much moisture of any kind and will not take glycerine either. July is a good month for deciduous plants.

Light Colours Most preserved foliage goes dark brown. Lighter colours result from putting the foliage, *after* preserving, in a sunny or very light window for a week or two.

Use with Flowers Preserved foliage can be used in water with fresh flowers as it is not harmed by the water.

A semi-permanent arrangement of preserved foliage can be kept in place for many weeks with one or two fresh flowers added from time to time. This is a great time and money saver. An arrangement in winter of florists' flowers looks much less bare when a few preserved leaves are added and often means that fewer flowers need be bought.

(*Left*) Dried and preserved plant material arranged in a Georgian copper tea-urn (*Right*) Preserved leaves, foxgloves and chrysanthemums on a pinholder

Plant Material	Cut	Time	
Beech (green or copper)	June to August	10 days	Easy to preserve and most useful in arrangements. It may need to be done annually as warm rooms can shrivel it.
Laurel	Any time but mid-winter	1 month or longer	Gives very dark almost indestructible leaves of a leather-like texture. Single leaves can be wired and used separately after treatment.
Eucalyptus	Flower shops in spring	2–3 weeks	Shades of purple and grey not brown. Should be very fresh when purchased. Longlasting.
Sweet chestnut	June to August	10 days	Pale brown. Good wired singly.
Oak	June to August	2 weeks	Pale brown. Oak apples usually stay on.
Whitebeam	June	10 days	One side goes brown the other stays grey.
Foxglove seedheads	June to July	2–3 weeks	Place in mixture when there are still one or two flowers at the top of the stem. Good for tall stems in an arrangement.
Rose leaves	July to August	2 weeks	Preserve on a woody stem. Sometimes a dark green colour develops.
Solomon's Seal	After flowering	1 week	Graceful curves.
Ivy with berries	When ripe	At least a month	Interesting berries for variety.
Fatsia Japonica (Japanese aralia)	Any time but mid-winter	Indefinite 2–12 weeks	Excellent leaves for use and almost indestructible. The leaves can be submerged in the mixture and, if not, must be mopped with it on the outsides (both sides). The leaf absorbs moisture slowly and will dry out if this is not done.
Aspidistra	Any time	12 weeks or longer	Well worth the wait—graceful pale brown leaves. Mop as above.
Dracaena (houseplant)	Any time	12 weeks	Mop as above.
Ivy leaves (large)	Any time	4–6 weeks	Submerge or mop. Very useful.
Fatshedera (house or garden plant)	Any time	4–6 weeks	Submerge or mop. Good shading of colour and a useful leaf.

Other plants to try
Foliage:

Camellia	Ferns (very mature)	Grevillea robusta
Cotoneaster	Peony	(house plant)
Mahonia	Bergenia	Maidenhair fern
Magnolia	Box (long time)	Elaeagnus
Clematis	Tulip tree	Helleborus corsicus

Seedheads:

Verbascum	Sycamore	Water iris
Plantain	Teasles	Old Man's Beard
Chestnut burrs		Catkins

These should be preserved when green.

Flowers:

Hydrangea (when mature but not dry)
Young lime (foliage removed)
Eryngium (see holly) the variety alpinum is good.

Bracts:

Molucella laevis (Bells of Ireland) when mature and with
foliage removed.

All plant materials preserved with glycerine are most useful and give great rewards for little work.

DRYING BY HANGING

The results are more fragile in most cases than preserving with glycerine, but this method is of good use for some flowers and seedheads. Pick on a very dry day when the flower is young and not fully open. Seedheads can be picked when beginning to dry on the plant. Tie in bunches so that the flowers do not crush each other and hang in an airy dry place for 2–3 weeks. Drying quickly in a dark place gives the best results for colour and there may be only a slight variation from the colour when fresh. Leaves should be removed as they only shrivel and retard drying. Here are some suitable plants:

Flowers	*Seedheads*
Amaranthtus candatus	Hollyhock
(Love-lies-bleeding)	Nigella
Acanthus	Clematis
Artemesia ludoviciana	Acanthus
Spiraea	Day lily (green stage)

Drying by hanging

Echinops (before flowers
   open)
Achillea (excellent when
   mature)
Eryngium
Pussy willow (in bud stage)
Liatris
Golden rod
Sedum
Larkspur
Delphinium
Allium
Globe artichoke
Heather
Lavender
Anaphalis
Polygonum

Angelica
Aquilegia (Columbine)
Allium
Dock (or Sorrel)
Cow parsley
Poppy
Teasles
Verbascum
Chinese lanterns
Iris (green stage)
Agapanthus
Honesty (slip off outer
   cases)

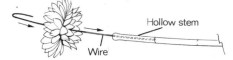

Wiring a straw flower

Grasses and Cereals These dry well by the hanging method. When gathered in the spring they remain green. Later in the year they are gold in colour. Ornamental grasses can be grown from packets of seed, such as Squirrel's Tail (*hordeum jubatum*), Hare's Tail (*lagarus ovatus*), large Quaking Grass (*briza maxima*) Job's Tears (*coix lachryma*), *setaria glauca*.

Annual Everlasting Flowers This sounds like a contradiction of terms but it refers to seeds which can be grown outside or in pots indoors giving papery flowers which are everlasting. Sometimes florists sell the flowers. They include helichrysum, rodanthe, xeranthemum, ammodium, statice and acroclinium. Cut as they begin to open and tie in bunches and hang to dry as above. When dry cut off the stem of the disc shaped flowers and push a florist's wire through the centre of the flower. Turn a small hook over at the top and draw this into the flower. The wire 'stem' can then be disguised by slipping it into any hollow stem. The seeds are listed in seed catalogues.

DRYING BY PRESSING

Flat plant material can be dried by placing between news-papers under a carpet or a pile of books. This method gives good colours but the results are very fragile. Suitable leaves are:

ferns	ivy	maidenhair fern
bracken	sweet chestnut	sumach
maple	beech	raspberry
iris	montbretia	cherry
gladioli	virginia creeper	

Any 'flat' or nearly flat flowers can be pressed. The plant material should be left for at least 3 weeks.

Hydrangea This can be dried by hanging but better results occur if the flowers are left to dry in $\frac{1}{2}''$ water in a container. They should be picked when papery in the centre. Do not add more water when it evaporates. Heather, variety H. E. Beale, does well in this way and retains its pink colour.

Foreign dried plants Flower shops often have a good selection of these in the winter. Examples are lotus seed pods from the East, agave seedpods from Spain, wood roses from Honolulu, banksia from Australia, proteas from South Africa, okra from America, poppyheads and palm leaves (embryo and mature) from Italy.

Cones All types of cones give interesting form and texture in an arrangement. They soon dry naturally. They are awkward to put into an arrangement unless they are wired but this is not difficult. Slip two florists' stub wires either side of the lower scales so that the wires are hidden. The wires should be parallel to each other. Twist the cone, which twists the wires. Then turn the wires down and round each other. Several cones can be wired together in a cluster. The wire is then pushed into plastic foam or plasticine (see mechanics) or can be wound round a stick for impaling on a pinholder.

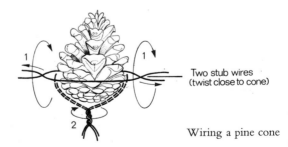

Two stub wires (twist close to cone)

Wiring a pine cone

Gourds These can be grown or bought. If grown, leave the gourds on the plant until very ripe, usually at the first early frost. They are also ready for cutting when the stem begins to shrink a little. Cut with a 3"–4" stem. Handle gourds very carefully or they bruise. To prevent rotting from mould or fungus sperm, they can be wiped with disinfectant. Place the ripe gourds in an airing cupboard for 1–4 months. When completely dry they are very light in weight and pale beige in colour.

Soft berries These do not dry. They can be kept for longer if sprayed with hair lacquer or varnish. They can also be dipped in a mixture of equal parts of shellac and methylated spirit.

Artichokes These can be dried impaled on a pinholder. The stems are short and a longer stem can be made by wiring to a stick. They are beautiful sprayed gold for Christmas.

BORAX, SAND, ALUM, SILICA GEL

The results can be very beautiful though fragile when flowers are buried in these drying agents. It is however a skilled job needing infinite patience. It is not a new process, it is known that flowers were dried in sand in the 14th century. Flower heads are buried in any of the above and completely covered. The flowers are best treated separately in boxes or tins with lids. The box is then placed in a hot cupboard from 2–7 days. Colours are well retained. Suitable subjects are:

roses	daffodils	primroses
dahlias	narcissi	zinnias
African marigolds	daisies	marigolds
arums	Christmas roses	gloriosa daisies
fungi		

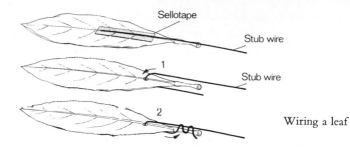

Sellotape

Stub wire

1

Stub wire

2

Wiring a leaf

MECHANICS FOR PRESERVED AND DRIED MATERIAL

1. Glycerined materials can go into the normal mechanics used for fresh plant material.

2. Dried plant material should not be placed in water unless the ends are dipped in melted candle wax or nail varnish. The easiest mechanics for dried materials are pin-holders for heavy stems, plasticine, chicken wire and dry plastic foam for thin and medium stems.

3. Single leaves often need a false stem of wire. Florists have stub wires in varying gauges. The stub wire can be placed on the back of the leaf and then held in place with Sellotape or a wire can be pushed through the leaf just above the place where the stem joins it. Bend it over for about 2″ and wind the short end round the wire below the leaf including the leaf stem if it has been left on.

USES FOR DRIED AND PRESERVED PLANT MATERIAL

In arrangements They can be used together with fresh plant material or on their own. There need be no lack of colour although the colours are quieter and more mellow than fresh plant material. Since the colour is not so dominant, various textures should be used to give interest, such as rough, smooth, downy, shiny, prickly and so on. It is also good to vary shapes to give interest. Wood combines well with dried and preserved materials.

A picture by Ivy Israels
using plant material
dried by pressing

Pictures Plant material which has been pressed very flat for at least three months, can be made into beautiful pictures, glassed and framed. The plant material is attached on the underside to a piece of coloured heavy paper with double sided sticky tape. It is important that the pressed plant material is as fine as tissue paper and really dry or the colour is not fast. It is advisable anyway to keep the completed picture away from strong light. The design should be tried first before anything is stuck in place. Place the 'picture' in a frame from a junk shop or take it to a framer.

Plaques and swags Three dimensional plant material can be made into beautiful everlasting decorations. A simple method is to cover a piece of hardboard with fabric, using a light fabric for dark plant material and dark fabric for light plant material. Mitre the corners of the fabric and glue on the back of the board. Stick gummed paper around the rough edges. Place two curtain screws in the back for hanging up with picture cord. On the right side of the covered board

(*Left*) Adding cement from a tube; (*Right*) The completed three dimensional picture by Eileen Caisley

work a little cement from a tube into a pile. Stick in plant material adding more cement if necessary, until the design is complete. The cement dries in about half an hour so it is wise to plan the design before starting.

Pegboard makes an excellent base for a swag or plaque. Cut into an interesting shape and then glue on the plant material with clear quick-drying glue. Cones and other wired material can be wired on through the holes in the pegboard. Various shapes and textures should be used. The natural surface of the plant material is more attractive but for further preservation the swag can be sprayed with varnish.

Plastic Cone Shapes Cones of a type of plastic foam which does not take water can be obtained from florists. Seedheads and leaves can be pushed into these shapes, wired if necessary, to make an attractive permanent decoration. Cones always seem to take more plant material than one expects, so save a lot in a box before beginning the decoration. The cone can be covered first with glycerined foliage secured with pins or small hairpins. The seedheads are then pushed through the leaves.

Christmas decorations Dried and preserved plant materials can be sprayed with gold, silver, copper or any of these mixed, for lovely results at Christmas. The fun is well worth the money spent on the paint. The plant material can be completely covered but occasionally just a touch of spray is beautiful. Do protect furniture and walls when spraying.

(*Left*) Glueing plant material to pegboard; (*Right*) A completed wall plaque by Sylvia Pullen

7

Nature's Sculpture

Wood that has been exposed to the natural elements of wind, water, sun and fire can become very beautiful when cleaned and treated. It is called driftwood but this does not necessarily mean that it has been in water. The term refers to any weathered wood, including large and small chunks, roots, crosscuts of trunks, bark, stumps and branches without leaves. Wood can be used in an arrangement for height and line, as a feature, as a base or container, and to hide the mechanics. Few flowers are needed with it and in many cases it looks wonderful standing alone, looking as effective and artistic as a piece of modern man-made sculpture.

It is interesting to realise that every piece is unique. The beauty of driftwood is ageless and easy to live with, fitting into any home setting. There is also a strange feeling of comfort with the thought that much of it is older than ourselves. The knowledge that it is the work of nature and not another man-made object makes wood so much more acceptable to most people than artificial plant material.

FINDING WOOD

This may seem a problem if you live in a city but trips to the coast or country for a holiday or for the day, give opportunities to look. Flower shops sometimes sell driftwood but it is more fun and more satisfying to find your own. Of course it does not jump in front of the car and say 'Here I am'—a walk is necessary, but searching for wood always gives interest to a walk and sometimes a family game. The British Isles are a wooded part of the world and there are many happy hunting grounds. You very soon develop 'the seeing eye'.

The best time to hunt is usually just after winter storms and before the undergrowth of summer covers it. Wood that has been in water is usually the cleanest and hardest, but lakes, sea, woodlands, bonfires and mountainsides all yield interesting pieces for the looking. If the 'hunting ground' has an owner or forester, it is wise to ask if the wood can be taken away. A small saw and a pair of secateurs can be useful to take with you.

Never bother to take home any soft rotting wood. It is not worth the trouble, as hard wood is essential. Colour and shape can be altered at home but nothing can be done with wood that is nearly all rotten. Small pieces of rotting wood can of course be removed as long as the remainder is hard.

Watch for bulls—if you are like me, treat all cows as bulls (just in case), or you may lose all your treasures in making a dash for it.

CLEANING

Unless you enjoy creepy-crawlies emerging from the wood into your spotless home, it is wise to give the wood a good scrub with detergent and water to get rid of the dirt and woodlice. Most wood is not fit to take into the house until you have done this. Grey wood must be washed gently as the grey is only on the surface and can disappear if it is scrubbed vigorously. After cleaning with soap and water dry outside, if possible in the sun, as this helps the colour.

There will nearly always be pockets of soft wood and odd pieces of bark to remove, especially on large chunks and roots. A small knife will soon get rid of this. When all the soft bits have been removed, give the wood a good brushing with a wire brush or sandpaper. You will be left with only hard wood. Cleaning can be a dusty job and needs to be done in an overall, preferably outside. It is a very satisfying occupation however. Again brush grey wood with a soft brush only. Sanding can be done professionally, This gives a velvety finish but it is inclined to be lifeless as many of the interesting markings and textures are also removed.

CHANGING THE SHAPE

After cleaning take a good look at the wood from all angles. Branches and roots, which often need little cleaning, may need some pruning to get a better shape. Larger pieces may be improved by sawing off some bits, or the balance may be better if the 'base' is levelled. Odd pieces of wood may need to be glued or screwed on so that the main piece sits at the correct angle. As little shape-changing as possible is best, since a scar is usually left which is not pleasing to look at and will need touching up.

POLISHING

When quite satisfied with the cleanliness and shape, the wood can be treated with wax for protection and for a good finish. Clear shoe polish or furniture wax are the most satisfactory giving a soft shine. Brush on, leave to dry and then brush off again, finishing with a soft cloth. You will be delighted with your piece of wood. Varnish can be used but it gives a hard look and it is not recommended. Apart from the beauty the waxed finish protects the wood when it is near or in water.

COLOURING

Most woods need no additional colouring. Occasionally the colour is dismal in which case there are ways of improving it.
1. Use coloured shoe polish instead of clear.

2. Place the wood in a bucket of water containing $\frac{1}{2}$ bottle of bleach and leave overnight. This lightens and yellows the wood. Wax or leave matt.
3. Use a wood stain and then wax.
4. Darken with linseed oil which preserves it and then wax.
5. Grey by soaking in very salty water overnight and then drying. Do this alternately for several weeks, during hot weather. This is a long job.
6. Greyness can be increased by painting with grey emulsion paint which should be wiped off before it dries. This needs care.
7. Put in a bonfire to blacken but watch that the whole lot does not burn away! Any wood blackened by fire should be waxed with black shoe polish which improves the finish and stops the charred part from dirtying everything it touches. This is not recommended for any but large chunks.

MECHANICS

Wood must be stable or it will fall over and ruin an arrangement. Once you know the methods and have decided which is the most suitable for your wood, it is really very easy.

Branches
1. These are best impaled on a pinholder if the wood is not too hard. If necessary split the end of the wood with secateurs to help it on to the pins.
2. Harder wood can have a hole drilled the diameter of a piece of dowel from a do-it-yourself shop. Push the dowel into the hole and glue if necessary. A long length of dowel fixed in this way to the wood can then be pushed into the container filled with sand or plastic foam for support. Short lengths similarly fixed will go on to a pinholder, and thick stems can have several of these false legs attached.

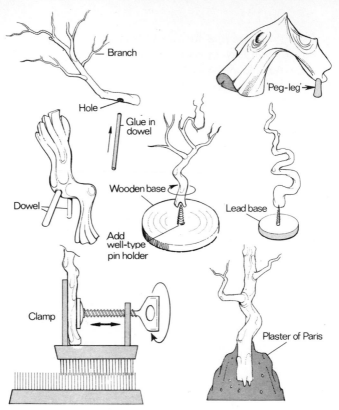

Mechanics for driftwood

3. Light branches and roots can be supported by plastic foam.
4. Clamps can be bought from flower shops which are excellent. These have a pinholder on the base facing downwards, which fits on to a regular pinholder. The clamp holds the branch firmly in most positions. It can be hidden with plant material, stones and so on.
5. Heavy lead bases are also sold with a screw sticking up in the centre. These are good for heavy branches and ivy vine. A hole should be made the size of the screw and the

lead base is just twisted in. If well balanced the branch should stay upright.

6. A crosscut of a trunk can be used as a base with a screw placed through it. This will also hold a branch in position as above. A well-type pinholder can be placed on the base for fresh plant material. Countersink the screw to avoid scratching the furniture or cover the head with felt. When making holes for screws at the end of the branch, watch the angle carefully so that the branch is not lop-sided.

Chunks These rarely need support as they stand alone. They may need the addition of a wooden leg to lift them into a desired position. This can be glued or screwed on. Nailing can split wood badly. Try to disguise the 'leg' by using similar wood or by colouring it to match the main piece.

Small chunks are invaluable for covering pinholders and will need no support. If you wish to add height to a piece it can be done with two peg legs of dowel.

Two or more small chunks of the same type of wood can be glued or screwed together and made into one interesting shape.

Roots These are normally soft and can be impaled on a pinholder. If very hard, use the same method as for hard branches.

Plaster of Paris from the chemist makes a good support for heavy roots. Mix the white powder with water. It sets in a few minutes so push the root in quickly, hold in position until it sets and the root will stand well. The plaster of Paris can be covered with moss or stones. Plasticine is poor for holding wood as it gives way when warm.

PLANT MATERIAL WITH WOOD

This should not hide the wood or there is no point in using

it. Wood blends equally well with brilliant colours and with mellow tones. I am sure that simplicity is the secret.

1. *Flowers* Striking flowers such as tulips, lilies and anthuriums are very effective but so are simpler flowers such as daisies and chrysanthemums. I have seen orchids used very effectively. Wood suits many flowers but just a few used simply look much better than a quantity which hides and detracts from the wood. A small well-pinholder can be concealed behind the wood to hold the flowers.

2. *Dried materials* These, especially the bolder forms, go very well with wood. This combination can make an almost permanent decoration for the winter. Plasticine or dry plastic foam can support the stems.

3. *Fruit* This blends well as it has the same sculptural qualities. Varying textures, shapes and colours give interest. Cocktail sticks pushed into the fruit will hold them in a group.

4. *Plants* These can be put in polythene bags concealed behind the wood.

Bases Most wood looks better on a base (see chapter 5). It need not be fixed permanently. Crosscuts or a piece of slate are usually the most suitable for an informal appearance. Polished slices are better for a formal grouping. Rush and bamboo mats are also useful.

ATMOSPHERE

It is surprising to see just how much atmosphere can be created by a piece of wood. It can set the imagination ticking very quickly so that one piece will take you to a stark mountain, another to a woodland or another, at a slanting angle, may give you a windy March day.

Used simply with a figurine with or without flowers, a story or scene is quickly created to provide a 'conversation piece'.

8

Using Few Flowers

Having spent eight years in a part of the world where it was too hot to grow any flowers successfully in the garden, I can well appreciate the difficulty of flower arranging without a garden. At the time I still felt a great need to have flowers in my home—perhaps even more than usual—but they were very expensive to buy from the refrigerator in the flower shop, and two or three was my limit, especially as they also had short lives in the heat. I began to build a collection of things with which I could stretch my few flowers into a larger arrangement and to my surprise found that the actual collecting became a great interest and a challenge which I have thoroughly enjoyed for years—and still do enjoy.

GOOD FRIENDS

Some objects seem to go with flowers and others do not. Anything made by nature always seems compatible but many man-made objects do not; such things for example as drug syringes, wigs of hair, cold potato chips and newspaper, all of which I have seen when an arranger has perhaps been carried away with a design for a specified subject in a show. However there are many beautiful figurines, glass bottles, elegant plates, pretty little boxes and so on, which can be used. Flowers are so beautiful in themselves that only things of taste are worthy of their company. Purely functional objects without beauty are not in keeping.

The Old Masters who painted flowers so beautifully in the sixteenth and seventeenth centuries knew what went well with flowers when they included shells, ribbons, birds' nests and fruit.

The objects used with plant material are for convenience called accessories.

ARRANGING WITH AN ACCESSORY

Whatever is used with the flowers should be part of the whole design and not an afterthought. A test of whether the accessory has been well integrated into the design is to remove it and see if you miss it. If so, then the accessory has been well used. Of course an accessory, such as a figurine, could be used quite separately on the opposite side of a mantelpiece, for example, but this is quite a different kind of grouping. I nearly always place the accessory in position first and work the plant material in afterwards—in this way it becomes an integral part of the design as you can't help taking it into account as you place the flowers in position.

WOOD

This most compatible and useful material has been well described in Chapter 7. Mention should also be made of lichened branches which can be found in damp places in the country and which last indefinitely. They are pretty used with one or two pink flowers and are effective sprayed with a little silver paint at Christmas time.

SHELLS, CORAL, SEA-FAN

One of the delights of a seaside holiday for me is beach-combing and for years I had collected shells, unable to resist them, without quite knowing what to do with them. Now exotic shells and coral can be bought in many places. Pet shops, amongst others, often stock them for aquariums.

Big Shells These can be used as containers, packed with plastic foam to support the flowers. They need something such as grasses or twisty hazel branches to give height, with a few flowers added.

Shells need height in the plant material or they appear very solid and it is attractive to see part of the beautiful inner surface of the shell. One beautiful flower makes a lovely centrepiece, floating in water in a large shell.

Fruit can also be 'spilled' from a shell and a bunch of grapes and two peaches have sometimes been my saving for a dinner table, when I have either forgotten to buy flowers or a crisis has arisen over cooking the dinner and time has disappeared.

Small Shells These can be grouped in a shallow container with one or two flowers on a pinholder on one side. They are particularly effective in a glass dish and look very pretty gleaming in the water. Small shells are also useful for covering pinholders.

Coral The lovely roughness of coral goes so well with smooth leaves and delicate flowers providing a contrast of texture and is again useful for hiding pinholders.

Coral Fan This looks rather like a skeletonised leaf but it is a type of coral and quite tough, although it can be cut and shaped with flower scissors. Many delicate colours can be bought but it does smell rather fishy although this seems to be forgotten when you see it with flowers. It can be held up on a pinholder if you cut any 'knob' off the bottom. If you want to leave this intact, then a small lump of plaster of Paris on the bottom will help it to stand. With a light behind it, coral fan can really look ethereal and it looks wonderful sprayed with silver paint and glittered for Christmas.

STONES

Stones, rocks, pebbles and slate are invaluable for hiding a pinholder and so easily available. A collection of different colours is useful, although black is the best. These together with several other colours can be found at Allonby on the North West coast. When grouped in a shallow container they should seem casual, but actually need careful arranging to make them appear part of the design.

CANDLES

These stretch flowers for a dinner party very well if they are used in the middle of the flowers. A small device can be bought from flower shops to support a standard sized candle. This can be pushed into plastic foam or on to a pinholder. The flowers can then be arranged around the candle. A pair of plastic foam saucers with candles and flowers is easy to arrange and attractive.

In order not to detract from the flowers, the candles usually look best if they are in soft colours. Cream, dark and light green and pale pink are good and by repeating the colour of the candle in the colour of the plant material a pretty harmony results. You can be dramatic, however, with a colour scheme such as navy blue candles and white flowers on a red cloth. Be careful that the plant material is kept well below the flame of the candle for safety sake, especially at Christmas time. When the candles are used for lighting, choose pale flowers such as apricot, pink, white, yellow, so that they show up well in the dim light.

PLATES

A beautiful plate is a good flower 'stretcher'. Holders can be bought at china shops on which to stand the plate upright. Then a plastic foam saucer or a well-type pinholder can be placed at the side of the plate, to hold plant material. This looks attractive if it follows the natural curve of the plate and

Metal holder ——

—— Add flowers and foliage

(*Left*) Using a candle; (*Right*) Using fruit

picks up one or more of the colours of the decoration. Pewter plates are effective at Christmas time used in this way with fruit, fir and a few fed roses. A small base under both plate and flower arrangement helps to draw the two together as one design.

FIGURINES

It is really fun hunting for figurines in antique shops, market stalls, attics and junk shops. Those made of bronze are the most beautiful but they are also the most expensive, and the colour is very compatible with flowers. Figurines can be found in wood, pottery, glass, china, jade and other metals. As with the plate, the mechanics and container can be placed at the side of the figurine or even behind it so that she appears in the centre of the flowers. The flowers and the figurine should complement each other in colour, style and shape. A dainty figure needs dainty flowers, a large one, large flowers, modern sleek figures need a similar arrangement and an animal or bird can look effective in a small scene from nature called a 'landscape' If you look at the figurine it will

(*Left*) A deer made of pine cones with driftwood, heather and stones
on a slate base; (*Right*) A dainty figurine arrangement

tell you the style it needs. If possible turn the figurine so that
it looks into the flowers and gives a greater sense of harmony,
and provide a base, which, as with the plate, draws the two
together.

GLASS

The use of windscreen glass has been described in Chapter
4, but large chunks of glass are effective gleaming in water
and can also be useful for covering pinholders. They can be
obtained from aquarium shops.

Beautiful glass vases and bottles which can be awkward for
holding plant material in themselves, can be used as accessories
with the plant material placed around them as for a plate.

FRUIT

We really do not use this enough with flowers or alone
as a decoration. It is such an economy as it can be eaten later
and even vegetables should not be overlooked. Faced with
a very V.I.P. dinner in January and with little money allowed
for the flowers by the particular organisers, on the small
tables I used oranges and lemons in groups, on ivy leaves

polished with salad oil. They were simple but striking and we soon sold them afterwards.

Fruit and vegetables have such unusual texture and colouring—think of shiny purple aubergines, rough avocado pears, downy peaches, elegant grapes in black, brown or green, shiny red and green apples, sharp lemons. There is a wealth of beauty and striking form, and a lovely grouping can be made with just a few of them.

Mechanics Fruit rolls around easily and gets out of place. The simplest way to hold it is with cocktail sticks, and piles of fruit can be built up in this way. A grapefruit can make a good starting point with the other fruit secured to it. Cocktail sticks do not normally damage fruit, so it can be eaten afterwards. Wire quickly spoils it.

A pineapple is a dramatic decoration. This is usually too heavy for cocktail sticks but it can be held in place on the top of a block of plastic foam by means of three or four butchers' wooden skewers pushed into the bottom of the pineapple. The sharp end goes into the fruit. Then flowers or other fruit can be added into the plastic foam at the sides. A spray of gold is effective on the leaves of the pineapple.

Grapes can be very graceful in an arrangement, especially flowing down one side of the container. Put a wire round the stem below a side stem and then attach this wire to a wooden skewer (or cocktail stick if the bunch is small). The stick or skewer goes on to a pinholder or into plastic foam. Artificial grapes are so realistic that they can be used amongst other fruits without people knowing the difference. This is also useful if the family are inclined to pick in passing.

Arrangements When the fruit is used alone use varying colours, textures and shapes for interest. Round fruit usually looks better in the centre with more elongated shapes on the outside.

Two apples will provide a rounded form for the centre with cupressus or evergreen and a few roses or carnations to make a long-lasting and economical design.

Leaves look pleasing with fruit and if long-lasting ivy or laurel are used they needn't be in water. Or better still, several preserved leaves can be tucked in amongst the fruit. They do seem to soften the rather definite outlines of the fruit.

As fruit does not have to be in water it can be arranged on a mat or base without using a container.

Flowers can be added amongst groups of fruit by means of a well-type pinholder or an orchid or cigar tube tucked under the fruit.

A Cone This is one of the most effective decorations for a special occasion. It is by no means a new idea as it was first used in the 6th century. The mechanics were different, as a central stem was probably used with the flowers bound to it, but the effect was the same.

Cut the corners off a large block of soaked plastic foam and place on to a pinholder (the type for plastic foam) on a container. Cut short pieces of evergreen and press the stems into the foam, covering it almost completely. Pittosporum and cupressus can often be bought at a flower shop. Push cocktail sticks (or halfsticks) into small fruit and then through the evergreen into the plastic foam. Suitable fruits are small apples, crab-apples, small pine cones (these can be wired, see Chapter 5), plums, damsons, apricots. Even garlic is effective. Then a few flowers can be added. They should be rather flat in shape such as single chrysanthemums (Bonnie Jean is white or yellow, Tuneful is bronze), or small roses (Carol is pink but there are yellow, red and flame varieties). The stems should be cut to about 1″ and pressed through the foliage into the foam. You will find that less flowers and fruit are needed if the foam has been well covered with foliage.

(*Left*) Roses, apples and cupressus in an antique container; (*Right*) A completed cone of fruit, flower sand foliage by Molly Duerr showing the method on the right

This is a semi-permanent arrangement as dead flowers or over-ripe fruit can be removed and replaced. The evergreens conserve the moisture in the cone but a regular spray of water helps to keep plant material fresh.

When I want a cone to last a long time I wrap it in a polythene bag before inserting the plant material. This does take a long time however as holes may need to be made in the polythene with a sharp metal skewer each time that plant material is inserted. The whole decoration can be made with dried or artificial material. Small pieces of dried hydrangea, achillea, straw flowers, pine cones and any small seed heads can be used. In this case cover the *dry* plastic foam with preserved leaves such as beech. The leaves can be secured with a pin or small hairpin. For this purpose flower shops sell ready-made cones of foam which does not hold water. Artificial Christmas materials and baubles on wires make a lovely cone decoration. But if you prefer fresh plant material the baubles can be used in wet foam to give a Christmas look.

101

9

Design Centre

Flowers are so beautiful in themselves that you may well wonder whether they need 'arranging'. Dropping them into a vase of water may be all that is necessary. The answer to this is that by displaying any beautiful object well, attention can be drawn to its beauty and sometimes a particularly lovely quality can be emphasised. Cleverly chosen surroundings can make a great difference. A painting looks better with good lighting and a harmonious background; sculpture looks wonderful against a sky, the space around making the form so much clearer; fine furniture looks at its best in elegant surroundings and so on.

Dorothy Riester wrote: 'A good flower arranger is one who sees, who discovers nature and places her discovery in such a light that others may see it too' and Picasso said: 'I want to help the viewer discover something he wouldn't have discovered without me'.

By understanding how to arrange and display plant material you and other people can become more aware of the colour of a rose, the shape of a lily, the texture of a peach, the curve of a branch.

The second reason—and a very practical one—is that to arrange flowers is sensible economy because two or three flowers well displayed can be more effective than many bunched together in one mass where the shapes and colours blur together.

ENJOYMENT

It really is important that you enjoy arranging the flowers you have bought or grown. The joy soon vanishes if you lose spontaneity and become frustrated with trying to do the impossible or failing to reach the desired result, and you feel like throwing the whole lot out of the window, container included. This rarely happens if you know the simple basic skills of conditioning and mechanics and if you understand the reasons for some arrangements looking awful and others beautiful.

I believe the secret is to arrange them quickly and to avoid labouring at the job. Chopping and changing the stems around will not usually help the arrangements and the flowers will look as tired as you feel. Instead, put the flowers in and then leave it. If the result is not to your pleasing when it is finished you will always have the consoling thought that it will be dead and finished in a week and can be thrown out. You will do a lot better next time. A bad painting or book is a lot more difficult to get rid of than a bad flower arrangement. Although the transient nature of fresh plant material has its drawbacks it has also the advantage of impermanence, and this is partly why it is such a fascinating art—one is continually inspired to capture its fleeting beauty. So do relax and enjoy yourself with your flowers.

PLAYING WITH PLANT MATERIAL

This sounds strange but getting to know the nature of the material you work with is important in any art. Plant material is not as malleable as clay, paint or other media. It has its own way of growing and as Brancusi wrote: 'You discover the spirit of your material and the properties peculiar to it. Your head thinks and follows the thoughts of the material'.

The qualities of plant material can only be realised by looking closely at it, playing with it, combining it in the hand with other materials. I like to spend time playing and then put it into the container quickly so that I don't lose sight of the qualities I have noticed.

It may be a colour combination that is striking, an interesting rough texture which may need a smooth one near it to exaggerate its quality. It may be a fascinating shape or line which will interest people.

It is a mistake to work against your plant material—to try to do an arrangement of straight lines with curving material or to bend material that is usually straight. Even if you are able to force it into position it will probably go where it wants when your back is turned!

Unless you are doing an abstract design most plants look better arranged according to their habit of growth. Flowers do seem to have personality. Gladioli for example are dignified upright flowers and look their best used upright in a container. Horizontally they appear unnatural, blown down in the wind. A soft, curving trail of ivy looks attractive trailing over the rim of a container and not forced into a straight line elsewhere. Foliage with short stems looks best in the centre of a design without unnaturally lengthened stems.

RULES

There are no rules except when you are arranging flowers in a competitive flower show where you can only win a prize by keeping to the rules set out in the Show Schedule and by adhering to the definitions which it uses. Otherwise there are no 'musts' or restrictions and you should do what you enjoy. Helpful guides to good display are something different and can help you to select plant material and show it off well, and these you can follow or not, as you wish.

SELECTION OF PLANT MATERIAL FOR YOUR HOME

This can be difficult—where do you start to cut in the garden or buy in the shop? Often as a result of not knowing, too much is cut or bought which is a waste of flowers and money. You may have no choice—you may have to use what is in the garden, what you have been given or what is available in the flower shop. If you do have a choice, these are the main considerations:

1. *Buy flowers you like*, you will enjoy them more.
2. Think of the place where you are going to use them in your home. If you have a large bare wallspace for example you may need tall or large flowers but if you want to look down on a few flowers on a small coffee table, then freesias or small roses will be the answer. In other words, think of the size of the place where you will put the flowers, and the size of the room.
3. Think of the *lighting*—a dark place needs yellow, white or tints of colours but a light position can take blues and violets and greens. Candlelight is very dim and needs very light colours—blues and violets vanish. White fluorescent lighting can make all reds look like mud but it is good for blues, and electric light shows off reds and oranges to advantage.
4. *Backgrounds* can really help flowers, so think of the wall against which the flowers will be seen. A plain wall is easy although (for example) you may not find white flowers showing up against a white wall. If your wallpaper is very decorative it is better to pick one of the colours that is in the paper to use in the flowers.
5. Think also of your available *containers* and what goes in them—if you have invested in 'earthy' coloured containers instead of bright colours, or in bases combined with well-type pinholders then you have no worries.
6. If you are arranging for a special *event* then the type of occasion influences your choice. At a dinner party, people look at your flowers closely and they should be clean, fine specimens without greenfly (which could hop into your guests' soup). At a cocktail party most people are

busy moving around and the flowers are not closely seen but they give a festive atmosphere and tall gay ones may be the most suitable so that they are at the same height as people's eyes. Certain events such as christenings or golden weddings may call for certain colours. A teenager's party may be the time for psychedelic colours or flowers with bold forms.

7. The *style* of the room needs consideration—simple bold styles of flower arrangements suit modern homes whereas massed designs suit the traditional home.

8. A decorative gap in a room can be supplied with flowers. For example—your one bright pink cushion will have a 'mate' if some bright pink flowers echo the colour.

COMBINING SHAPES IN PLANT MATERIAL

Sometimes only one shape is available but if you have a garden, or have collected plant material in the country, if you have preserved and dried or if you have a florist who has a large selection of plant material, then you have a choice of shapes to combine in a design. I used to find this very confusing until I was given an easy formula which I have found invaluable over many years. Think first in terms of what your own eyes do when they look at a flower arrangement—they travel around it stopping at various places and then moving on again. So it follows that your eyes are happiest if they have help in moving around the arrangement and also can stop now and again to rest and enjoy something.

In order to move the eye around and into the design, plant material that more or less follows a 'line' is good. It can be straight like this / or curved, ∫ or it can be formed by shapes in a row like this 𝟖 . All these cause your eye to move along. This shape O holds your eyes in one place. So a combination of these two shapes—lines and rounds can move your eyes around and hold them for a while also. To jump from a line straight to a round /O can give the eye an

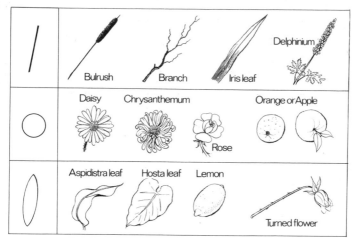

Basic shapes

unpleasant jar and an inbetween shape can soften the effect, ⟨𝟢⟩ I call this shape a stepping stone. It neither moves nor holds the eye strongly. It is a harmoniser drawing the two unlike shapes together.

These three very simple basic shapes can be used together to make a very satisfactory design, ⟨|⟩⟨𝟢⟩⟨○⟩ If you study plant material you will find that *generally speaking* it follows one or more of these shapes. For example —bulrushes, delphiniums, bare branches, iris leaves and long tight buds follow the line shape—they move your eyes along. Examples of plant material which approximates to a round shape are open dahlias, roses and chrysanthemums, daisies when seen full face, fruit such as apples and oranges, foliage of sempervivum (houseleek) and London Pride. Examples of stepping stone material are half open buds, flowers turned to their sides, lemons, foliage of *many* kinds. Some plants have these three shapes all on the one plant. Roses have slender buds on the tops of stems for lines, open flowers for rounds and foliage for stepping stones. Gladoli are the same when the lower flowers are wide open. An arrangement of wide open dahlias with nothing else can look very 'blobby' being all rounds and your eyes have trouble moving around the design. So when you only have rounded flowers to arrange, it is helpful to turn most of the flowers to the side.

These three shapes are the basis for most designs using a combination of shapes. Lines draw your eyes in and around the design, rounds momentarily hold your eyes, and the stepping stones are the helpful in betweens. The number of each shape used, depends on the style of design. The simplest most streamlined modern designs use only one type of plant material for each of these basic shapes: for example, bare branches for lines, open roses for rounds, and rose foliage for the stepping stones. Mass designs use more of each, particularly the stepping stones.

GUIDES TO GOOD FLOWER ARRANGEMENT

The Use of Space We know night because of knowing day, youth because of age, shape because of space. Without space, shape is not defined and a shapeless mass results.

Anne Morrow Lindbergh wrote in *Gift from the Sea* 'For it is only framed in space that beauty blooms. Only in space are events and objects and people unique and significant . . . and therefore beautiful. A tree has significance if one sees it against the empty face of the sky, and a note of music gains significance from the silence on either side. A candle flowers in the space of night. Even small casual things take on significance if they are washed in space like a few Autumn grasses in the corner of an oriental painting, the rest of the page bare.'

Some styles of flower arrangement use far more space within the framework of the design than others, but whatever the style some space is needed around each flower, branch or leaf so that it can be clearly seen—unless you are bunching many small flowers together to make a larger round shape.

The Japanese have a charming instruction—'Leave room for the butterflies to fly through the flowers'.

Turning Flowers The full beauty of flowers can be admired if flowers are turned so that they can be seen at differing angles. Sometimes the backs and sides of the flowers are just as beautiful as the front and sometimes more so, as in the arum lily. The back of a poppy has great interest and a daffodil is more striking from the side. The flower paintings of the Dutch and Flemish old masters show flowers at many angles and the interest people had in every part of a flower in those days.

When flowers appear on a plant they are normally to be seen facing in all directions, So it is following nature's own lead, to arrange flowers facing different ways.

Shortening stems Flowers can be seen better if the stems are all of different heights. The flowers don't then crowd each other, vie for attention. It is a mistake to cut all flower stems very short as the result is a squat-looking design, but if none are cut the result is often top heaviness and a view of stems rather than flowers. Some long stems, especially if they are curved, give grace to a design and far less material will be needed when they are used both long and short. The long ones give height and width and the shorter ones interest in the centre.

These three simple guides apply to most styles of flower arrangement whether of one type of flower or of several types of plant material.

LINE AND MASS ARRANGEMENTS

Styles of flower arrangement fall into these two broad classifications. The style of the Western World, has, up until recently, been arrangements of massed flowers, fruits and foliage, using little space within the actual design. The

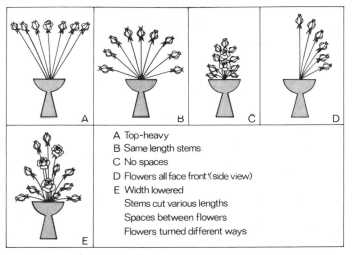

A Top-heavy
B Same length stems
C No spaces
D Flowers all face front (side view)
E Width lowered
   Stems cut various lengths
   Spaces between flowers
   Flowers turned different ways

ABCD—Design faults: E—Correct

Japanese have been masters of line designs in all the arts for centuries and flower arrangement is no exception. Line plant material is often dominant and there is much space within the design. From these two styles others have developed. The characteristics of a line design can be described as:

1. Dominant line plant material.
2. Restraint in plant material.
3. Space used within the design so that the lines can be clearly seen.
4. Interest in the qualities of individual plant material.

Mass arrangement characteristics are:

1. Little space within the design.
2. Interest in quantity rather than the quality of individual plant material—the effect of colours blended together and of shapes combined.
3. Little dominant line plant material and more rounds and 'stepping stones'.
4. Interest in the outline of the solid flower arrangement rather than of individual lines within the design.

Simply speaking it is the difference between the beauty of one branch of apple blossom and of the beauty of a bunch of garden flowers.

MAKING AN ARRANGEMENT

A line arrangement The simplest design to start with is one using little plant material. This does not mean little in size (this is often harder to do than a big arrangement)—but in quantity. My advice is to pick one or even two interesting branches either bare or stripped of most of the leaves and to impale these on a 2″ or 3″ pinholder in a baking dish which is deep enough for water to cover the pinholder. If possible choose a container which is earthy in colour inside and out—brown, grey or green. These branches are the lines which draw your eye into the arrangement. As a very rough guide the branch should be a minimum of $1\frac{1}{2}$ times the width of the container. This is because a shorter branch will make the container seem bigger and more important than your carefully picked plant material. Usually you can go higher than $1\frac{1}{2}$ times the width especially if you are using a thin branch and a heavy looking container. If you are using a tall and not a low container, then a minimum $1\frac{1}{2}$ times the *height* of the container is a good guide. But use your eye not a tape measure and do go higher if you want to.

Having placed the branch or branches in position—they usually look best if the top turns into the design rather than out and away from it—then add two rounded flowers such as open roses turned at slightly different angles. If you put them in a space rather than against the branch they will not hide the shape of the branch.

'How long should the stems of the roses be?' is probably your next question. The top flower looks well balanced if it is placed about halfway between the top of the branch and the bottom of the container. Try it in place and then cut the stem. Cut less rather than more at first as once cut, the stem cannot go back on again. The other flower needs to show up well also. Cut the stem so that the flower ends up just below the other one, but in its own space. Two leaves or sprays of foliage can be added wherever you feel they are needed. Keep the stem ends of all the plant material close together on the pinholder to get a sense of radiation from one spot which is more attractive than having stem ends far apart on the pinholder. One or two stones can cover the pinholder. When these flowers are dead try the branches in a different position and use another variety of flower for a different effect. You can go on doing this at little expense for some time, studying the plant material and the spaces around it.

A Mass Arrangement When you have plenty of plant material —it need not be all flowers, it can be mostly foliage—try a bigger arrangement. It really does not matter where you start the design although many people find it easier to start with the tallest stem and place it about $\frac{2}{3}$ of the way back on the pinholder or plastic foam. This tall stem should be roughly $1\frac{1}{2}$ times the height or width of the container which should be deep to hold enough water for the plant material. The place where this stem is placed on the mechanics becomes the radiation point for all the other stems. I like to place something towards the back at this stage, and I do mean pointing *behind* the container. Then add two pieces at either side of the container to give width. If they are shorter then the first tall stem the appearance will be better. A short stem pointing forwards can then be positioned. Your stem will then have formed a framework which goes into all three dimensions— height, width and depth. Many people have the impression that flower arrangement is similar to painting a picture but it is far more like sculpture for both use three dimensional material whereas painting is two dimensional. Flower arrangement is more related to painting with regard to colour, than shape.

(*Left*) A simple line arrangement using arum lilies (*Right*) a small mass arrangement of garden flowers

Choose one or two rounded flowers, the biggest you have to give a central point to the design in the front. These flowers usually look best facing full front. Some people call these flowers 'the centre of interest'. Their position should be roughly half-way between the top of the tallest stem and the bottom of the container for the balance to look correct. The two flowers can be slightly turned in different directions. If some plain short stemmed foliage is placed encircling these two flowers, then they have a plain background to offset their beauty.

Now you can add other plant material. Flowers should be gradually turned away from the central ones. Taking the first tallest stem as the pivot point they turn gradually around so that from the front of the arrangement the flowers at the back actually face backwards. This means the design also looks attractive seen from the side. Make sure every flower is in its own space and that the stems are different lengths and add some foliage, if possible, to give a dense feeling at the centre of the design. Foliage can be used instead of flowers and only two or three flowers need be used in the centre.

Mass arrangements need a clear outline—it can be triangular in which case start with line material. It can be round or oval in which case turned flowers or stepping stone material will make a better start. I like to use curving material at the side, giving 'arms' which are soft like those of ballet dancers rather than stiff like those of gymnasts. Mass arrangements usually look the most attractive in containers with a stem such as urns. These lift the design up so that there is space below it and the side stems of plant material can be clearly seen. In these mass designs the smallest flowers are normally used at all the extremities.

SCALE

This refers to the sizes of *all* the things you use in the design. A mouse looks ridiculous with an elephant and a slender grass looks out of scale with a huge dahlia. We feel the need for a reasonable relationship between the sizes of everything used together. This includes the flowers, foliage, container, base, and even the room where the arrangement is placed.

TEXTURE

There are many fascinating textures in plant material. There are downy bulrushes, shiny camellia leaves, rough pine cones, silky flowers, to name only a few. Some things have a silky feeling when touched but *appear* rough because of the formation of the petals and the way they break up the light. Plant material which is, or appears, rough should be placed against textures with a smooth appearance. Each enhances the other. Two rough textures together do nothing for each other, just as a fussy feathery hat looks better with a

(*Left*) Poor use of scale (*Right*) Better use of scale

plain dress than with a frilly dress. *Contrasts* of texture look better together than *similar* textures. Sometimes many of the textures used in a design are rough as in a design of dried and preserved plant material, and here a metal or pottery container with a slight sheen can provide the needed contrast in texture. If everything in the design is smooth (for example silky roses and beech leaves), a stone or piece of coral can provide a contrast with its roughness. Whenever a design is of only one shaped flower or of one colour, then textural changes in the plant material can provide needed interest.

COLOUR

There is so much to learn in colour theory that it is not possible to include many details in this book. Here are some general guides:

Variation There are thousands of colours in the world and by really looking at plant material you become aware of colours you had not realised existed. It is interesting to make a collection of foliage. There will be many greens—pale and dark greens, yellow and blue greens, greyed greens and just greens. Arrangements look alive when you take advantage of these variations. For examples at Christmas time red carnations are often used with dark green holly. In colour this can be a dull arrangement until some yellow-green ivy is added, when the whole colouring seems to spring to life. In any colour scheme nature's variations are attractive, and a leaf or flower with more than one colour—a turning Autumn leaf for example—has much beauty.

Quantity People wonder 'How much of this colour and how much of the other?' A general guide is that to most people's eyes, smaller rather than larger amounts of brilliant colour are more pleasing. So in any group of colours, use least of the most brilliant colour and most of the paler or duller colours. Nature shows this—there are many greens, browns and blues around us and fewer of the brilliant flower colours.

Nature's Colour Schemes Ideas for colour schemes are all around us if we have time to look and become aware of them. A pansy has variations of violet with a touch of brilliant yellow and a holly bush shows bright red berries against dark green leaves. Hydrangeas combine lovely soft colouring together and a croton leaf contrasts of light and shade. Sunset or dawn can give wonderful ideas for colour schemes and even a snowy day shows how brown and white can be combined. The sea and stormy days show us duller but still beautiful colour and the colouring of birds and butterflies is fascinating. Such things as these are far more inspiring than painted blocks of colour on a page.

Repetition I have found that almost any colours may be combined together if they are repeated and not used alone. The old masters used many colours together and the flowers are very varied—but a colour repetition gives harmony, each spot of colour has a friend. It is worth studying the paintings of good artists to help you with colour harmonies and you can try designing an arrangement in the colours characteristic of an artist when you have plenty of plant material—Gauguin's rich colours, Constable's brown and greens and so on.

Surroundings Flowers do not like competition in colour and everything but the flowers should normally be more subdued —base, container, accessory, background. This does not mean that you should not use one of the colours in the plant material but a greyed version of it is a better foil for the flowers. For example with bright pink flowers, a bright pink velvet base would compete for attention, a greyed pink or a 'mushroom' pink is more pleasing.

Advancing and receding colours Some colours give the illusion of moving towards you—these are orange, red and yellow. They are good colours to use in a big room. Blues and violets recede and in a small room can make the walls seem farther away, while in a small hospital room they are probably more soothing to a really ill patient than reds and oranges. Green is neutral in movement. If violet is used in the centre of an arrangement it will disappear at a distance and the arrangement appears to have a hole in the middle.

Colour temperature Some colours are warmer to look at than others. Red and orange give a reminder of fire and heat. Blue and green are cool colours and are associated with woodland, sky and sea. An arrangement in reds and oranges is very cheering on a bitterly cold day just as an arrangement of blues and greens is cooling in a heat wave.

Colour and surroundings Lighting and surrounding colour can alter the appearance of colours and it is almost impossible to isolate an arrangement. Lighter colours appear larger than darker colours in a design, which shows up considerably more if there is a great contrast between it and the background. A light yellow arrangement will show up much more against a dark brown wall than against a light orange wall for example.

Luminosity This is the quality that makes some colours appear more visible than others in poor light. White and yellow are the most visible and black and violet the least. So in a dark church white and yellow arrangements will be seen more clearly. This also applies to colours with a lot of white in them which are called tints.

HARMONY

The most pleasing designs are those in which every part seems to belong to every other part and to have a sense of relationship. This includes flowers, foliage, accessories, container, base and background. Harmony comes with

An arrangement in the style of Dutch flower paintings

trial and error, with looking at pictures of flower arrangements and at other peoples' designs. A rough piece of driftwood for example is not in harmony with a velvet covered base. It is more in harmony with a crosscut of wood or a base of slate. The relationship may be one of colours, associations or texture, but whatever it is, if all the parts work together in a design for a feeling of unity, the design will be harmonious.

BALANCE

If your arrangements look top heavy, bottom heavy or lopsided the visual balance is wrong. The actual balance will probably be quite stable but your eyes may be pulled too much to the top or bottom of a design or to one side rather than the other, because there are too many eye-catching things not evenly distributed. Larger shapes, brighter colours, longer lines, shinier textures, rounded shapes all draw the eyes more than their opposites. If a container is very large and dominant try something big and bright high in the design or a very tall stem to attract the eyes up and away from the container. If a design appears lopsided it may be that a brilliant flower on one side needs something to balance it on the other side—not necessarily the same type of flower but something equally eye-catching. If you mentally imagine a central axis horizontally across the middle of a design and another vertically down the centre then try to see that your eye is attracted equally to either side of these lines. Modern styles which do not rely on symmetrical shape for balance are built up in this way. Place a piece of plant material on one side of a container and then add another piece (something different) on the other. If your eye is still attracted more to the first placement, then add a third piece of plant material to the second. Go on building up the design, balancing and unbalancing with other plant material until you have enough in to be pleasing. Usually stop before you think you should.

When you do not know where to put the next piece of plant material it is usually time to stop. Most people put far too much in an arrangement and then the flowers do not show up and the design is fussy. When you have finished the arrangement go away and forget it. When you have a little time sit down with a cup of coffee and look at your design. Ask yourself some simple questions to help you assess your own design.

1. Do the flowers look fresh?
2. Are the mechanics stable and hidden?
3. Is everything clean and well groomed?
4. Does the plant material suit the container?
5. Is there anything I could take out and not miss?
6. Do all the parts of the design belong to each other?
7. Is everything clearly seen in space?
8. Does the design look balanced?
9. Can I see flowers at different angles?
10. Is everything in scale?
11. Do the colours blend and suit the background?
12. Have I tried something different this time or is it the same old thing?

My advice is not to change anything unless it is to remove something small. Most designs go really wrong once you start to make major changes. Leave it and next time you make an arrangement you will quite naturally improve any faults you have found.

TAKING IT FURTHER

When you have become practised in making a simple line design and a mass arrangement you may like to venture into other variations of these styles. You may also feel that the time has come for some guidance from other people. Your local Education Officer can tell you of evening classes available in your district. If you would like to join a Flower Club, there are more than a thousand throughout the British

Isles. The address of your area organisation can be obtained from the headquarters of the National Association of Flower Arrangement Societies (or NAFAS as it is known), 21a Denbigh Street, London, S.W.1. Some flower clubs meet at night and others during the day, usually once a month. At these clubs you will meet other people who are interested in flower arrangement and in growing plants. Some will be expert and others will be learning like yourself, and most clubs welcome men and women—some of the most outstanding flower arrangers are men. Each month there will be a demonstration by an expert of about seven arrangements and he or she will talk about the plants used and the design, giving helpful advice. Sometimes there will be practice meetings.

Flower shows both of horticulture and flower arrangement are organised in many parts of the country and news of them will appear in the local press. These may lead you to an interest in competitive work both decorative and, for a stimulating change, interpretative where you give your version of a story, an atmosphere, a landscape, a mood and so on, with plant material.

The local library will have books on flower arrangement by many authors.

Your interest may lead you to study period styles—those of the Egyptians and Victorians are particularly interesting. You may be attuned to the modern and enjoy abstracts, or you may choose to study the relationship existing between flower arrangement and the other arts. One of the fascinating things about flower arrangement is the many other interests that it inadvertently leads you happily into—pottery, antiques, gardening, history, colour and so on. Personally I enjoy every part of this fascinating and absorbing interest which has so much to offer. Gardeners and flower arrangers are a happy, friendly group of people who share a wonderful contact with nature, a contact which many of us need.

Appendix I

Plant Material for Flower Arrangement

This list could be endless, and fill volumes. I have therefore selected only plant material that lasts well in water or will preserve or dry for winter use, is easy to grow anywhere—and, if out-of-doors, is suitable for a *small* garden.

My list also includes 'wild' plant material that can be collected for nothing in the countryside, and don't forget that in this case the collecting is in itself both a pleasure and an illumination.

As flowers can be bought all the year round at flower shops, foliage plants predominate in the list. These are the best buys for flower arrangement if one has to be selective, because foliage is hard to come by in shops and yet easy to grow or gather. It is also excellent for making flowers go a long way so that fewer are needed for an arrangement.

These lists are basic and further varieties can be added later. Many are evergreen for all the year round use. Those that preserve are marked with a 'p'.

Evergreen

Aucuba japonica variegata ('*Maculata*') Shrub. Spotted laurel.
    Very useful   p
Bergenia 'Sunningdale' Hardy perennial which goes red in
    winter. An indispensable foliage plant for plain circular

leaves (cordifolia) and obovate (crassifolia). Good for covering mechanics.   p

Camellia japonica Shrub. Needs acid soil and a sheltered site when young. Moves house when you do.   p

Cupressus macrocarpa 'Lutea' Shrub. Rough texture.

Elaeagnus pungens 'Maculata' Shrub. Green and yellow streaked foliage. Good colour in winter. Remove plain leaves which appear.   p

Escallonia x *iveyi* Shrub. Slightly tender, needs shelter. Long stems of foliage.   p

Fatshedera lizei Shrub. Sheltered place and shady.   p

Fatsia japonica Shrub. Needs shelter. Invaluable for large leaves to preserve.   p

Helleborus argutifolius (*corsicus*) Hardy perennial. Bold leaves, best in open but sheltered position.   p

Ilex aquifolium 'Golden King' (holly) Shrub or tree (variegated green and gold.   p

Ligustrum ovalifolium 'Aureo-marginatum' Semi-evergreen. Golden privet.

Lonicera japonica 'Aureo-reticulata' (Japanese honeysuckle) Climber, evergreen or semi-evergreen. Long sprays yellow-green foliage. Warm position.

Mahonia japonica Shrub. Elegant leaves. Sweet smelling flowers.   p

Phormium tenax Shrub. Tall sword-like leaves. Sheltered position.   p

Skimmia japonica 'Foremanii' Shrub. Light green foliage. For bright red berries needs a male plant *S. japonica rubella*.   p

Tellima grandiflora Perennial. Low growing round leaves with good veining. Ground cover.

Thuja occidentalis 'Rheingold' Shrub. Golden rough texture, turning orange-bronze in winter.

Vinca major variegata (periwinkle) Ground cover. Good trails of foliage. Cut back in spring.

Acer pseudoplatanus 'Brilliantissimum' Deciduous tree. Slow grower but worth the wait for pink leaves in spring. Any soil.

Alchemilla mollis (Lady's Mantle) Hardy perennial. Yellow green flowers, lovely with anything. Medium sized round leaves. Easy to grow and good ground cover.   p

Allium sphaerocephalon, *A. porrum* (leek), *A. cepa* (onion) Round flowers for drying.

Anaphalis Triplinervis (Pearl everlasting) Hardy perennial. Small white flowers for drying.

Arum italicum 'Pictum' Hardy perennial. Low growing with leaves marbled green and white which can be picked under the snow. Feed well for large leaves.

Astrantia major Hardy perennial. Unusual small flowers which last well.

Berberis thunbergii 'Atropurpurea' Hardy deciduous shrub. Mahogany coloured leaves in long sprays.

Coryllus avellana 'contorta' (Harry Lauder's Walking Stick) Shrub. Interesting twisted branches. Quick growing.

Curtonus paniculatus. Corm. Giant montbretia flowers, pleated sword like leaves. Seedheads dry.   p

Eryngium (Sea-holly) Hardy perennial. Dries well. The variety 'Alpinum' glycerines, flowers included.   p

Euphorbia epithymoides Hardy perennial. Bright yellow bracts in spring.

Iris Hardy perennial. Sword-like leaves. *I. foetidissima* has orange seeds.

Hosta Hardy perennial. Good in city gardens. Invaluable foliage. Any variety.

Hydrangea Deciduous shrub. Flowers to dry and glycerine   p

Lunaria (Honesty) Hardy biennial. Seedheads for drying and good leaves.

Nicotiana Annual for flowers.

Phyllitis scolopendrium (Harts Tongue fern) Cool shady spot. Watch snails.

Physalis franchetii (Chinese Lanterns) Perennial. Dries well.

Polygonatum multiflorum (Solomon's Seal) Perennial. Graceful long stems.   P

Rosa rubrifolia Deciduous shrub. Grey leaves in sprays.

Rhus cotinus 'Folius Purpureis' Deciduous shrub with dark red foliage. Plant against the setting sun for lovely autumn colour effect.

Salix 'setsuka' Deciduous shrub. Fasciated willow. Quick growing. Interesting winter stems for lines.

Sedum 'Autumn Joy' Perennial. Good flower heads for rough texture at all stages of growth.

Senecio cineraria 'White Diamond' Shrub, not evergreen in cold places.

Winter cabbage and kale (ornamental). Hardy annuals.

To Collect in the Country

Bulrushes, cut when green, for drying

Pine cones

Beech for preserving

Hazel catkins, long-lasting

Ivy, long-lasting, preserves

Spruce, long-lasting

Seedheads, for drying

Grasses, for drying

Magnolia, long-lasting, preserves

Oak for preserving

Bracken for pressing

Lime flowers for preserving

Old Man's Beard for preserving

Rhododendron—preserve

Whitebeam—preserve

Hornbeam seeds—preserve

Sorrel for drying

Heather for drying

Driftwood

Beech

Oak

Sweet chestnut for preserving

Ferns for pressing and preserving

Pussy willow for drying (pick before pollination)

Broom, tie in circles, soak 2 hours in cold water, dry 2 days in the airing cupboard and untie for swirls.

Florists' Long-Lasting Flowers

Achillea (Yarrow) (dries)
Agapanthus (African lily)
Alstroemaria (Peruvian Lily)
Anemone
Anthurium
Baccarat roses
Carol roses
Chincherincherees
Chrysanthemums
Clivia
Echinops (Globe-thistle) (dries)
Eremerus (Fox-tail Lily)
Eryngium (Sea-holly) (dries)
Freesia
Gladioli
Gerbera
Ixia
Lilies (of all kinds)
Marguerites
Orchids
Peonies (in bud)
Pyrethrum
Ornithogalum
Statice (dries)
Straw flower (dries)
Strelitzia
Sweet William
Trollius
Tulips (in bud)
Zinnia

Foliage for Growing Indoors

These have been chosen as they grow quickly and will not show gaps if the occasional leaves are removed.

Aspidistra elatior (Cast Iron plant) Long-lasting in water. Excellent preserved. Can go outside in summer shade. p

Camellia japonica Good in tubs. p

Cyclamen Useful foliage when flowers are dead.

Fatshedera lizei Long-lasting. Preserves well. p

Fatsia japonica Long-lasting. Preserves well. p

Geranium Good leaves.

Grevillea robusta Good for preserving. Quick growing. p

Hosta undulata Force in spring.

Ivy. Long lasting. Spray with water. p

Nephrolepsis (Ladder Fern)

Philodendron scandens Long-lasting, quick growing.

Polystichum setiferum 'Divisilobum' Pretty fern.

Yucca filementosa Long-lasting sword-like leaves.

Tradescantia Grows quickly.

Appendix II

PLANTS FOR SITUATIONS

Sunny positions All cacti and succulents; very easy to care for, little or no water in winter for the majority and moist compost in summer. Sansevierias; keep on the dry side at all times. Chlorophytum; keep moist, feed regularly and put on into new compost each year in spring. Dracaena marginata; pot on annually and keep the compost only just moist, an easy plant to care for. Crotons; many sorts in many colours, maximum sunlight. Never allow to dry out and feed regularly. Many of the Bromeliads do well, particularly the variegated pineapples, or ananas.

Sunlight other than very bright midday Saintpaulias (keep water off leaves and flowers), poinsettias and most other flowering indoor plants. Flowering plants should all be kept moist and have dead flowers removed regularly. Variegated hederas, tradescantias and variegated peperomias also do well in these conditions.

Good light, no direct sun Almost all indoor plants will do well in this sort of situation, except for those mentioned earlier which definitely prefer a sunny position.

Shaded situation There are few plants that do really well, though there are plants that will tolerate these conditions:

aspidistra, philodendrons, ferns, Ficus pumila, monstera, marantas and platycerium.

Gas heating Flowering plants generally do less well. Best subjects are those with thicker leaves, such as rubber plants and sansevierias. However, experiment will show that, where rooms are well ventilated, a surprisingly large number of plants may be grown quite successfully.

Temperature Excessively hot or cold conditions present problems for almost all plants, so only recommended easy ones are advised for such conditions. Fluctuating temperatures are also problematical, and only the toughest plants are likely to survive. An even temperature in the region of 55/65°F is best for most plants.